PRAISE FOR HIDDEN HEARTACHE

What do you do when your husband's addiction to pornography leaves you shattered, betrayed, and devastated? Who do you turn to in the aftershock? In *Hidden Heartache* you'll find the heart of a friend you can trust and the hard-earned wisdom of a woman who has been there. For the past fifteen years, Jody Allen has courageously lived the truths written on each page—truths that will guide your heart away from despair and toward the heart of God, showing you how to let Him meet your greatest needs. With biblical wisdom and practical steps, each call to courage will help you heal, grow, and find hope after betrayal.

— RENEE SWOPE, AUTHOR OF *A CONFIDENT HEART: HOW TO STOP DOUBTING YOURSELF AND LIVE IN THE SECURITY OF GOD'S PROMISES*

Hidden Heartache feels like a daily roadmap to help you journey toward wholeness and healing after the devastation and disappointments associated with pornography, betrayal, and divorce. Jody's authentic story allows you to feel like you have a best friend, yet expert to guide you through your own process for healing and hope. Jody's use of God's Word and prayer is the spiritual nourishment needed to take each step.

— LISA J. ALLEN, CERTIFIED LIFE COACH, SPEAKER

No one wants to talk about pornography. It's vile and destructive. It is also a powerful addiction that destroys people and devastates relationships. It is time for this emotional cancer to be brought into the light and faced head on.

Jody Allen has done just that in her book, *Hidden Heartache*. Jody personally experienced the powerful grip of pornography as it destroyed her marriage. Instead of allowing the pain to overwhelm and silence her, Jody powerfully shares the pain she has experienced as a result of pornography's grip on her husband.

In her book, Jody is transparent and authentic. She shares her life in a candid way that offers the reader steps to take, ways to make a plan for restoration. In sharing her story, Jody has brought hope to what can seem to be a hopeless situation – and reminds us that God alone can bring healing and victory.

— MARY SOUTHERLAND, SPEAKER AND AUTHOR OF NUMEROUS BOOKS INCLUDING *LIFE IS SO DAILY* AND *ESCAPING THE STRESS TRAP*

Jody's desperate prayer for a breakthrough in her marriage reminds us that God hears and answers our prayers even when His answer is not what we expect. Jody invites us to acknowledge our pain while applying Ephesians 6 to put God's armor on and use His weapons in spiritual battle. She shares practical ways to lean into Jesus, our Sufficient Savior, and apply the truth of the Bible, watching it become more than words on pages, but the experienced reality of faith lived courageously in the face of adversity. We can learn from her choice to believe, trust, hold on to, remain steadfast, forgive, and that choice becomes a living path of hope and healing.

— MONA L. DOOLEY, M.A., LPC

When it comes to marriage, pornography is a silent serial killer. It will kill the respect in a marriage first. Then it kills trust. Intimacy is also a victim, as is confidence. And sadly, in many cases, the marriage itself is the final casualty.

Jody Allen has been there and done that. Her husband's pornography addiction wrecked and eventually killed her marriage. In her book, *Hidden Heartache,* Jody has turned her hurt into help by analyzing what happened and recommending a better way. Her honest and practical approach is so refreshing. This book is worth the read.

— DAN SOUTHERLAND, PASTOR, AUTHOR OF *TRANSITIONING: LEADING YOUR CHURCH THROUGH CHANGE* AND *CHAIR TIME: A SIMPLE LIFE-CHANGING WAY TO PRAY*

What a beautiful story of hurt, love, growth, and resilience. With a mix of truth, vulnerability, rawness, and humor an amazing journey is shared with others. With practical and needed exercises and reflections for healing, *Hidden Heartache* is a great testimony of faith and courage!

— STEFANIE J., LMFT, CSAT, CMAT, CPTT

HIDDEN HEARTACHE

Finding Courage When Your Husband Struggles with Pornography

Jody Allen

Published by Willow Springs Press

Printed in the United States of America.

Library of Congress Control Number 2024924632

ISBN 979-8-9920466-0-1

eBook ISBN 979-8-9920466-1-8

This book was originally published by Bold Vision Books ©2024

Edited by Larry J. Leech II

Cover design by Amber Wiegand-Buckley, Barefaced Media

Interior design by Alycia W. Morales, Story Inspirations

For my children. Always follow your God-given dreams. I love you.

CONTENTS

INTRODUCTION

We looked like a picture-perfect family. My husband had a respectable job. I was a stay-at-home mom of twins. We lived in a cute house, drove two old, but paid-for, cars and were proud pet owners of a somewhat obedient black lab. We took family vacations. We were leaders in our church.

And we were living a lie.

Not a blatant lie. Just more of a façade. Everything looked hunky-dory from the outside. Yet, unsaid and unknown issues lingered in the middle of carpool, bills, and cutting the grass. One day that façade came crashing down.

The lazy days of summer had ended, and we were back in the routine of school—getting up to alarm clocks, packing lunches, and tackling homework. My children were in their first week of fourth grade when I noticed one child wrestling with schoolwork. That struggle sent me searching for answers. I could have never known as I searched on that September Saturday that I would come head-to-head with a different struggle entirely.

I searched our computer looking for anything to help manage the necessary evil called school. I expected to find tips, ideas, and tried-and-true advice on how to help a floundering fourth grader. I expected to find what I needed and move to the next thing on my list. I didn't expect what popped up on my screen.

Pictures. Lots of pictures. Pictures of people I didn't know. Questions raced in my mind. Who are these people? Why are they on my computer? More importantly, where are their clothes?

My stomach sank. My heart thumped like someone hit it with a hammer. My world stopped but my brain darted from questions to panicked thoughts to disbelief.

After a moment, adrenaline kicked in, and I stepped into detective mode. Sherlock Holmes would have been proud. I hunted for more pictures by plugging in different camera brands. Nikon, Pentax, Sony, and others. With each search, more pictures of barely clothed strangers appeared on my screen.

When each batch of pictures popped up on the monitor, I felt the room closing in on me. I felt my whole world crumbling down around me. And I felt the picture-perfect facade cracking right before my eyes. I knew my husband had struggled with pornography in the past. We had walked that road several times before. But now? After countless therapy sessions, a strong support system, and promises to stop.

Tears stung my face. I felt alone, shocked, and unsure what to do next.

Sound familiar? Maybe your circumstances were a smidge different, but the experience was the same. You're crushed. Trust has been yanked out from underneath you. And you're left balancing a fragile marriage while spiraling between shock, anger, and sadness.

You are not alone. And you don't have to take this journey alone.

Chapter One

YOU'RE IN GOOD COMPANY

"I will lead the blind by ways they have not known,
  along unfamiliar paths I will guide them;
I will turn the darkness into light before them
  and make the rough places smooth.
These are the things I will do;
  I will not forsake them."
Isaiah 42:16

Acknowledging your situation is a significant step of courage. You have joined other Christian women whose lives have been turned upside down by their husband's pornography use. Plenty of women who have found themselves thrust into a world they thought only existed in the lives of others.

As it turns out, those women exist in our neighborhoods, in our churches, and even in our families. Women who are also walking this common but secret journey. You are in good company.

Your husband has a lot of company too. Two-thirds of Christian men view pornography monthly. Yes, *Christian* men. And, if these men have a significant other in their lives, two-thirds of women are affected by pornography. Two-thirds.

Think about your group of friends. It's possible two out of three are on a similar journey. Women who are sitting in our churches, raising families, leading Bible studies, and suffering from broken hearts. But they're not talking about it.

We don't have to look far to find pornography. Cell phones are portable porn machines. One out of five mobile searches is for pornography.

In your search to make sense of your life these days, you have likely heard well-meaning people tell you not to worry about your husband's porn issue because "it's just something men do." Implying that looking at women other than their wives is normal and acceptable. It's not. It may be acceptable in our culture, but it is not acceptable to our God.

The just-something-men-do crowd may think there is no harm in watching pornography. "It's not hurting anyone," they say. You and I know that's not true. Pornography hurts people. Some believe it's easier to rationalize porn than deal with it.

Our culture can rationalize porn to the end of time, but it cannot deny that porn addiction is a very real thing. Porn is addictive, just like alcohol, drugs, and gambling. When pornography captures men, they may do things they never thought they'd do. Lie about how they spend their time. Make excuses for staying up late. Pay hard-earned money to porn websites. With each lie or unwise choice, men chisel at the foundation of their family while risking their reputation and possibly their job.

No man woke up this morning and said, "I think I'll develop a porn addiction today." Of course not, but it happens when "just something men do" slides from a monthly, or daily, bad habit into an addiction.

Wherever your husband is on the porn spectrum, he needs help. And you need help. Sweeping the issue under the rug and hoping for the best won't make it go away. After the initial shock passes, you may think you're fine. Or that you don't need help since you're not the one with the problem. While that's somewhat true, his problem is now your problem. A problem that stirs up a lot of emotions.

When I discovered pornography on that Saturday, a whole list of emotions surfaced. Shock and hurt came first. But the overarching emotion that simmered beneath the surface was anger. Fear and shame weren't far behind, but I was pretty ticked off. I had to acknowledge that my life was not the picture-perfect one I dreamed of on my wedding day. I would like to tell you that my husband and I worked through all our issues, fell madly in love all over again, and are living happily ever after. That is not true.

Sadly, we are divorced. Nothing on this planet can prepare a person for the ripping apart of a family. Nothing. The shame I experienced when pornography was exposed pales in comparison to the shame that I experienced walking through divorce. Even as I typed this, I sensed a twinge of judgement. Maybe no one is actively judging me, but feelings of awkwardness and embarrassment bubble up within when three words come out of my mouth, "I am divorced."

A divorced woman writing this book seems like an unlikely combination. To be honest it would be easier to skip writing this book. Who wants to be humiliated all over again? I'd rather bypass the embarrassing and delicate nature of our situation and move on. But God just won't have it. Trust me. I've tried to let it go and move on. God has been too persistent to let me waste my pain.

Besides, He brought significant healing to my life, and I don't want to be stingy. I want to offer you the truths and tools that took me down a healthy path toward healing. These aren't secrets or an exhaustive list of magic things to make the pain go away. They are simply a collection of ideas you might find helpful to get you through your days. Or at least today.

I also feel a commitment to women with porn-addicted husbands. While we are vast in number, we are low on courage. I want to be the cheerleader that you need to help you take your next step. I want to be a voice that reminds you that you will make it. Yes, the journey will be hard, but you can get to the other side of this dark season and be okay whether your marriage survives or not.

So, this book isn't about marriage. It's about you and for you. But I do hope it impacts your marriage.

I wholeheartedly believe God can do miracles, even in shattered marriages. He is not bound by time, courts, or human hearts. He is above all and completely in charge. He wants healing for you and your marriage. Two healthy people can lead to a healthy marriage.

The truths and tools in the following chapters will lead to a healthier you, a more courageous you. A spiritually and emotionally healthy you that lives and loves well. Married or not.

If you're not married but are reading this because your boyfriend or fiancé is struggling with pornography, run, don't walk, to counseling to address these issues *before* you get married. Contrary to popular belief, pornography use doesn't go away when people say, "I do."

I speak from experience. My husband believed getting married would solve the pornography issue. It seemed logical but was not true.

We can agree on one thing that is true. Let's go ahead and say what we're both thinking. This is not fair. It's not fair that our husbands have taken their past and dumped it into our present. Pornography has been plopped in our laps like a crying baby, except we're the one crying. It's not fair that we have to spend our time, energy, and money on a problem that belongs to someone else. There are a million ways to spend our time and money. Pornography wasn't on the list.

I will admit that I lived the first thirty years of my life thinking life was fair. For whatever reason, I assumed if I followed God that He would make my life good, or at least tolerable. As it turns out, that's not in the Bible. Unfortunately, bad things happen to good people. You and I can attest to that.

Yes, you and I are victims of bad choices made by another person, but we don't have to live like a victim. Victims are powerless. We are not powerless. If you have trusted Christ as your Savior and invited Him to be the leader of your life, you are not powerless. You have the power of the living God to courageously fight this unwelcome battle. So, fight for your wholeness, your marriage, and your family.

To be clear, this book is not about fighting our husbands or a book slamming men. We have churches, businesses, and homes full of godly men who love Jesus. We seek healing for ourselves and healing in our relationships with others including the men in our lives.

This book is not a comprehensive study of pornography or a scientific look on how pornography affects the brain. It's also not a replacement for counseling. Please do educate yourself and find a qualified counselor.

This book is a story. Not just a story about a gal who has walked a hard road, but about a God who heals broken hearts. The pages you are about to read are a reminder that there is light at the end of this dark tunnel.

You can stumble through and be broken, or you can stumble through, be broken, and allow God to put you back together. He can take your broken pieces and make something brand new.

Your broken pieces may look different than my broken pieces. What I know to be true for all of us: the choices we make today and the next day decide where we'll end up next week and next year. The truth is we don't want to be here. But since we are, let's be brave and ask God to help us take each day and each step with wisdom and intention.

At the end of each chapter, you'll find an action step, A Call to Courage. A baby step to help you navigate your road, ground you in truth, or sort through your feelings. This is the practical piece we need to step out of shame and move toward healing.

To get started, grab a journal (spiral bound notebook, staple some paper together, or your phone). Record your thoughts, dreams, hurts, prayers, hesitations, verses that jump out at you, memorable quotes, important events, emotions, etc. There is no wrong way to journal. It doesn't have to be neat or perfect. Remember to date your entries. You'll want to go back and read what God has done.

If you're not the journaling type, no big deal. Grab your paint, markers, clay, pencils, or crayons and express your emotions, thoughts, frustrations, etc., to record your journey.

> Friendship is born at that moment when one person says to another: "What! You too? I thought I was the only one."
>
> — C.S. LEWIS

Chapter Two

CROSSING THE BRIDGE

When I am afraid, I put my trust in you.
Psalm 56:3

In 2019 I embarked on a journey to conquer my longstanding fear of heights. I'm not bothered by a Ferris wheel or airplane rides. For some reason, being 40,000 feet in the air doesn't bother me. But put me on the side of a mountain, and my heart races as I scramble for the low country.

To tackle my fear of heights, I decided to walk across the mile-high swinging bridge at Grandfather Mountain. If you've never been, it's a great experience if you don't mind walking across a swaying chunk of metal positioned a mile above sea level. Nothing screams mental toughness for someone who struggles with acrophobia.

With you on my mind, I threw my laptop over my shoulder and tentatively stepped onto the bridge. Cautiously shuffling across the bridge, I pretended I was as brave as the next gal. My chest tightened while I walked farther away from the mountain over the valley below.

When I stepped off the bridge on the other side, I was greeted by large boulders with no guardrails. I gingerly took a seat on a rock far from the edge. I pulled my laptop out of the bag and looked up to see a stunning view of the Blue Ridge Mountains stretched out before me. The mountains went on for miles. The view was truly spectacular. I opened my laptop and started writing to you.

The wind gusted while I typed, but it wasn't windy enough to shut down a bridge, nor was it windy enough to shut down an act of courage. And you know what? I didn't die. I faced my fear and survived.

But conquering Grandfather Mountain didn't cause my fear to disappear. There will be other mountains to climb and fears to face. Bravery is moving forward in spite of fear. Bravery is taking steps into the unknown even when it's hard.

You're at a bridge you never thought you'd cross. Never in a million years did you think you'd be dealing with your husband's pornography issue. Never. Yet here you are. It's hard, embarrassing, painful, and downright scary.

Do you remember the old saying, "We'll cross that bridge when we get to it?" Well, the bridge has come to us. While this bridge may not have been our choice, we get to decide how we want to cross it or *if* we want to cross it.

Truthfully, you could stay put on the safe side and do nothing. You could choose not to have the difficult conversations, not to work through the painful feelings and sweep it all under the rug. You can pretend your life is fine. That is certainly an option.

But what happens if you decide it's too difficult or too humiliating to address the issue of pornography? Will your relationship improve? Will you be emotionally well? Are you willing to live a lie?

The "if" route isn't our best option. If we settle for the "if" option, we will likely find ourselves bitter and angry with a lifetime of regret by the time our hair turns gray.

Instead, I want to invite you to walk courageously into the unknown. To have the hard conversations, to do the work in counseling, and allow yourself to grieve. It is possible, even if it's difficult, to come out on the other side whole and dare I say, happy.

The other side of the swinging bridge called my name. I packed my laptop to search for a less dangerous place to write. I nervously shuffled back across the bridge. As I placed my foot on solid ground, I glanced back to marvel at my courageous accomplishment.

A sign at the entrance caught my eye: "Load limit: 40 persons on bridge at one time."

Forty. That number rings a bell. The number forty is mentioned several times throughout Scripture. In Noah's day, rain flooded the earth for forty days and forty nights. The Israelites wandered in the wilderness for forty years. Goliath taunted the Israelites for forty days. Jesus was tempted in the wilderness for forty days. And the list goes on and on.

The number forty indicates a time of hardship or trial testing our limits and challenging us to live beyond our ability. These trials beckon us to live in the capacity we can only find by relying on Someone greater than ourselves. Sounds like our situation.

Just like Noah and the Israelites, you and I are living in 'a forty moment.' We are facing the trial of a lifetime. A trial requiring us to live beyond our capacity. A trial causing us to seek God in ways we never knew we needed.

Millions of Christian women just like you are facing a forty moment. They stand at the bridge, trying to decide if letting the cat out of the bag is worth the risk. Not all women will decide the potential results are worth the effort. That doesn't have to be you. You can be the woman who courageously steps into the unknown even if your knees are knocking and the wind is howling.

It's scary. Unknowns always are. Since the moment you discovered or confirmed your husband's pornography issue, you have likely been living in the unknown, unsure of what tomorrow may look like.

Your thoughts may be taunting you about being rejected, divorced, not loved, or financially ruined. You fear if you tell someone what's going on, you'll be humiliated or dismissed. Or this was a big one for me—you'll never stop crying.

You don't have to stop crying to be courageous. Bravery isn't the absence of fear. Bravery is the presence of trust. Trust in a God who can take all things, scary, hopeless, and heartbreaking, and use them for our good if we let Him.

You get to choose. You can pretend the issue of pornography isn't an issue or you can courageously step on the bridge one baby step at a time. You don't have to take a giant step. Just one baby step today then another baby step tomorrow. And one day, somewhere down the road, you'll glance over your shoulder and marvel at the courageous journey you've walked.

But it starts with one step. The first step.

Your first step.

Be assured, God doesn't have a limit on the number of women He wants to cherish, scoop up in His arms, and guide on this journey. On the contrary, He has room for as many women who are willing to take the risk.

So, whether you avoid Ferris wheels or the edge of high mountains, I hope you'll accept this call to courage from a fellow bridge-crosser because the view from the other side is spectacular.

> The true courage is in facing danger when you are afraid.
>
> — L. FRANK BAUM, *THE WIZARD OF OZ*

A CALL TO COURAGE

Educate yourself about pornography. I know you'd rather put your head in the sand but knowing is equipping. You don't have to go overboard but research the signs of a pornography addiction or how pornography affects the body and relationships. Or what the Bible says about pornography and a few statistics.

Chapter Three

PRAY LIKE CRAZY

> "Then you will call on me and come and pray to me, and I will listen to you."
> *Jeremiah 29:12*

Forty-eight hours prior to my discovery I was home alone cleaning. At the time we had ten-year-old twins, so any time to myself was a gift to my introverted self, even if cleaning was on the agenda.

Being home alone in the evening was unusual. Our family did everything together. Trips to the mall, to get ice cream, or ride bikes. So, when my son had soccer practice, we usually went to his practices together. My husband would help coach and my daughter would take art supplies to draw. I went to gab with the other moms.

This particular Thursday night, however, I decided to skip practice to tidy up. Being alone gave me the opportunity to listen to whatever my heart desired. Maybe a good podcast or some '80s tunes or even a little silence. I'm not opposed to Vacation Bible School songs or listening to Jack and Annie tackle another adventure in *The Magic Tree House* series, but a grown-up can use some grown-up listening time.

I settled on a Chip Ingram podcast. Ingram is a Bible teacher skilled in simplifying difficult ideas. I'm a gal who can get bogged down with details, so I appreciate the simplicity.

In this podcast, Ingram taught on breakthroughs, not settling for mediocre when God has something far better than mediocre in mind for our lives. His passion for people breaking free from mediocrity was contagious. And his words quenched a thirsty longing in my heart.

For quite some time, I felt like I had been living an ordinary, run-of-the-mill life. Sure, there were some fantastic moments along the way but, by and large, we were average. It seemed like there was more. At least I hoped there was more. My life wasn't terrible but the day-to-day was a little too humdrum for my taste. Mediocrity had crept in and settled into my marriage.

To be truthful, my marriage was less than mediocre. It seemed impossible and completely hopeless to me. I remember countless times sitting at Chick-fil-A with my friend Jenn rehashing the same sad and hopeless feelings about my marriage. I couldn't believe we had gone from "I love you, dearly" to "I tolerate you, barely."

Around the time of our fifteenth wedding anniversary, I had lost all hope in our marriage. The selfishness and rejection had finally pushed me to the point where it didn't matter to me if we lived like roommates for the rest of our lives. I was exhausted from the effort to try and make things work.

During those hopeless times, I struggled to believe God could answer my prayer that involved the choices another human would need to make. Could God really change a person's heart? Had my husband's heart become too hard? What about my heart? Could God really bring back love?

A couple of months after our fifteenth wedding anniversary, I came to my senses. I realized giving up was not an option. I needed to take care of myself even if nothing in my marriage changed. I decided to pursue counseling. Not for my marriage but for me. I was seeking emotional and spiritual wholeness for me even if my circumstances never changed. I'm the only person I can change anyway. But I would welcome the superpower of changing others.

I found a Christian counselor and mustered the courage to send her an email. That brief email was the beginning of a journey that would prepare me for the dark days that lay ahead.

While I listened to Ingram that Thursday evening, he posed a question: "Do you want this fall to be like every other fall or do you want a breakthrough?" *Yes! Yes! Emphatically yes!* I longed for a breakthrough. My heart was aching for change.

By this time, I had several months of counseling and a lot of years of Bible study under my belt. I really wanted to believe God could break through the mediocrity of my life. That there was more to this life than what I was living. I was desperate for change.

Mind you, I had been desperate for change plenty of times before. Maybe you have too. I will never know what makes one plea of desperation different from the next. I only know that God responded to this plea differently than the others.

You know how you really want something, but you sleep on it and the desire goes away? Well, that didn't happen this time. I went to bed that night with a breakthrough on my heart and Ingram's question tucked in my journal. The next morning, I continued my plea for a breakthrough. Something. Anything.

When I pondered what a breakthrough might look like, I dreamed of a healthy marriage full of ministry. I dreamed of opportunities to use our pain to minister to others. I dreamed of financial freedom, a loving family, and all the things little girls dream of.

I was so serious, I considered fasting. I have fasted a few times and understand why it's considered a discipline. I admire people who fast because, to be honest, I like to eat. But I decided to take the plunge. I would start fasting on Monday. You can't start something like that on a Friday. Every diet, exercise program, and anything that requires sacrifice starts on Mondays. But God was gracious to this peanut butter lover. He answered my prayer before Monday.

God answered my plea for a breakthrough in forty-eight hours. Two days. By Saturday afternoon my world had turned upside down. The day I discovered pornographic pictures on my computer. The day my husband moved out. The day my life changed.

Frustratingly, God didn't answer my prayer the way I would have liked. I'm not going to lie to you, I questioned God. I wondered what in the world He was thinking and why He chose to answer that way.

While it may not be how I would have chosen to answer, He did answer, nonetheless. That alone brings me hope. The God of the universe, the One who created the earth from nothing, holds the stars in the sky and knows the number of grains of sand not only heard my prayer but He actually answered it.

Sometimes it's easy to think our problems are too insignificant for God. I mean, He has the whole earth, the weather, and billions of other people to manage. Why would He listen to me? Why does He care about my mortgage payment, my knee pain, or my broken heart?

God is not unaware or unmoved by our hurts. He not only hears our cries for help, but He answers them. He is involved in the intricacies of our day-to-day lives, even if we don't notice or care.

Several years before the discovery, we were on a family vacation in the mountains. We stayed at a friend's house, where we had stayed many times for our anniversary. We didn't usually go there in the summer, but this year we needed an inexpensive vacation, and our friends were gracious enough to share their house. We hiked, fished, played in the river, and stumbled upon a waterfall to climb. I didn't fish. Too many slimy things.

One afternoon we were inside taking a break from the zillion-degree North Carolina heat when we heard a loud thud. A sweet little hummingbird had somehow overlooked the dust and dirt and flown full speed into the sliding glass door. We hopped up and went over to find the poor guy stunned by his run in with the door. He was so dazed, we were able to pick him up and hold him. Well, I didn't. My husband did. His body was small and delicate. We stared at him in awe that something so small had so much detail. Amazing, really. Eventually, he came around and back into the woods he went.

The God of the universe, the One who holds that tiny bird in His hand, says that you and I are worth more than many sparrows. (See Matthew 10:31.) He knows our hearts are broken into millions of pieces. He knows our secret longings and our heartaches. He's big enough to take our anger and frustration. He is not put off by our cries for help or our tears.

Because of who He is, we are free to bring our deepest aches and worst fears to Him. He doesn't just listen, He answers. Sometimes without fasting.

> Prayer does not fit us for the greater work; prayer is the greater work.
>
> — OSWALD CHAMBERS

A CALL TO COURAGE

Our prayers do not fall on deaf ears. God hears every desperate prayer poured from your broken heart. He is not annoyed by you or uninterested in your hurts. He wants to hear from you. Let's be brave and pray big.

Beth Moore reminds us in her Bible study *Jesus, the One and Only* that "God does not have some limited supply of power, requiring that we carefully select a few choice things to pray about. God's power is infinite. God's grace and mercy are drawn deeply from the bottomless well of His heart."

Maybe you're in such a hard place you don't know what or how to pray right now. The words just aren't coming. You are not alone. Sometimes praying other people's words can be helpful.

So, why not use God's words? I'm a big fan of praying scripture. If you're not already praying scripture, let's do that today. Fill in the blank with your name or someone else's name.

When __________ is weighted down with weariness and burdens, remind her that she can come to you and you will give her rest. (Matthew 11:28-30)

Thank you that you know the plans you have for __________, plans to prosper her, not to harm her, to give her hope and a future. (Jeremiah 29:11)

Help _________ to trust in you with all her heart and not lean on her own understanding.
(Proverbs 3:5)

Be the stronghold of _________ life so that she has nothing to fear.
(Psalm 27:1)

Give _________ a new heart and put a new spirit in her. Take out her stony, stubborn heart and give her a tender responsive heart.
(Ezekiel 36:26)

Cause _________ to hunger and thirst for righteousness, so that she can be filled.
(Matthew 5:6)

May _________ know the truth and be set free.
(John 8:32)

Help _________ to stay alert, watching out for her enemy who is prowling around like a roaring lion, looking for someone to devour. Help _________ to stand firm against the enemy and be strong in faith.
(1 Peter 5:8-9)

I praise you because you are greater than _________ heart and you know everything.
(1 John 3:20)

Cause _________ to take captive every thought to make it obedient to Christ.
(2 Corinthians 10:5)

Assure _________ that Christ has set him free. Give him the courage to stand firm and not be burdened again by a yoke of slavery.
(Galatians 5:1)

Chapter Four

THE GIFT OF CHOICE

> If any of you lacks wisdom, you should ask God, who gives generously to all without finding fault, and it will be given to you.
>
> *James 1:5*

Do you have a list of 'I'll nevers?' I'll never wear socks with sandals. I'll never be a mall walker. I'll never watch *Murder, She Wrote* reruns.

I'll never is our emphatic way of stating that at no time will we ever be or do a particular thing. Yet here we are a few birthdays later wearing clothes we never thought we'd wear (hello, Spanx) and watching the Weather Channel for entertainment.

Sometimes things happen that challenge our I'll nevers. Time passes, perspectives change, life experiences happen, and we find ourselves at a crossroad, one that challenges our I'll nevers and beckons a decision. A choice greater than Birkenstocks and socks.

Has your pornography discovery brought you to a crossroad? A crossroad requiring courage to make a decision that will affect the lives of the people you love. You may be able to put off some choices another day, another week, or another year. But eventually a choice must be made. We must answer the question: What am I going to do?

That is the question I asked myself that September Saturday. *What am I going to do?* For me, there was no waiting another day or another month to decide. My choice was clear but far, far from easy. The minutes that followed my discovery changed my marriage and my family forever.

I didn't need to wait another day because this was not my first experience discovering pornography during our marriage.

When Sam and I married, I had no idea pornography had been a struggle for him for years. He assumed, as do a lot of men, once he got married the desire for pornography would dwindle and life would be fine. It didn't, and it wasn't.

He didn't know it wouldn't go away, and I didn't know what to do when the issue of pornography came up. You don't know what you don't know, which is why education is so important. Because of my lack of knowledge, I wasn't equipped with tools to navigate the pornography road before me. To make matters worse, pornography wasn't talked about, or at least I didn't hear about it.

In our early married days of the late 1990s, I remember sitting on our love seat one Sunday after church and Sam voluntarily acknowledging his struggle with pornography. He said he wanted to stop. I said, "That's great." So, we moved on. In my naivety I assumed he stopped, and everything would be fine. I had no idea it wasn't that easy. Maybe he didn't either.

If I knew then what I know now, I would have chosen a different response. Hindsight really is 20/20 or at least clearer than the present. I can't change the hands of time or go back and re-do what has been done. All I can do is learn from the past, educate myself to change the future, and share what I know with others so they can choose a different and better path.

To be clear, I'm not taking responsibility for his actions but for my lack of knowledge concerning pornography.

Before kids appeared on the Allen family scene, we enjoyed having folks over for hangouts. Hosting a party was a no-brainer. I'd tap away on our computer to create paper invitations and drop them in snail mail to get the word out. Don't have visions of a sleek computer with lightning-fast internet. Think of a big, heavy computer that took up half the table space and ten minutes to boot up. But we did, at least, have a computer.

In preparation for a party, I searched our computer for an invitation I had started. The search brought up more than an invitation. I discovered a host of adult websites that had been accessed from our computer. *What?* I was caught off guard!

Even now, I can close my eyes and go back to the office in our first house with our huge computer perched on a card table and remember the feeling of the room closing in around me. *How could this be? We are happily married. Maybe it's just an accident.*

I kept searching. Looking at the time stamp on all the questionable websites. Looking for what I was sure to be a mistake. Looking for the good I knew was in my husband. I was devastated by my findings. The sites were visited at times when I wasn't home. I was crushed.

When he got home, I met him at the door. I took him by the hand and led him straight to the computer. I can't say I remember exactly what happened next. I remember lots of tears from both of us. We were both brokenhearted. I was devastated.

The loving, fun marriage I thought we had turned out to be a lie. Not only had he looked at the websites, but he had been deceptive by doing it while I was away.

Pornography was one thing. Deception was a whole different story. A telltale sign of addiction.

Again, my ignorance missed an opportunity to choose a different path. My lack of knowledge left the pornography issue for him and his men's small group to deal with. We had a great support system. We were involved in a home group. We were active in our church and had completed more than one marriage Bible study. I figured with all that support he would work through this issue and get back on track.

The fateful September Saturday, fifteen years later, made it obvious that pornography was still an issue. But this time, I had walked the road too many times to assume it would get better. This time I had to choose a different way.

With scary thoughts of the unknown swirling in my head, I

mustered the courage and reached for the phone. There would be no waiting until he got home this time. I would like to tell you that I got on my knees and prayed and heard a great word from God. I didn't. I just knew. I knew what had to happen. I knew I had to take a stand. I knew the answer to the question. I didn't know one single thing past that.

I dialed his number and when he answered, said, "You'll need to find somewhere else to live because you're not living here."

And that's what he did. He moved out that day and, sadly, never moved back in.

That was the hardest decision I had ever made. I knew asking him to move out would devastate my children and tarnish our picture-perfect image. But the time had finally come when a hard choice had to be made. A choice that required more courage than I had used in my lifetime.

Making hard choices can seem like it's disturbing the peace. Matthew 5:9 says, "Blessed are the peacemakers, for they will be called children of God." What it doesn't say is, "Blessed are the peacekeepers." There is a difference between a *peacemaker* and a *peacekeeper*. A *peacekeeper* keeps peace at all costs. A *peacemaker* pursues peace through the courage to make hard choices.

Let's not keep peace that's not worth keeping. I'm not suggesting we turn into troublemakers. We must use discernment and have the right motives. But sometimes the peace we're keeping isn't peace at all. It's simply a façade of peace covering a mangled mess of undealt with stuff.

Sam has told me on more than one occasion that my decision on that Saturday was the best thing that ever happened to him. Not the easiest, of course. My choice forced him to look at his pornography use for what it was. Addiction.

Knowing that, I often second guess my choice to not take a stand earlier. I kick myself wondering if I had made hard choices earlier would things have turned out differently. I will never know. I cannot live in regret or dwell on the 'what ifs.' I choose to move forward knowing I did the best I could with what I knew at the time.

Maybe you're at a crossroad asking yourself that same question:

"What am I going to do?" That question repeatedly rolls through your mind like a broken record. Or you're haunted with that question day in and day out as you go through the motions of a loveless marriage. Is it time to make a hard choice?

My answer may not be your answer. Your answer may be to start a conversation or ask a question or install a filter on your computer. Or see a therapist, find a twelve-step recovery program, or find a couples recovery program.

I know two things:

First, if you do nothing, nothing will change. If you're aching for change or a breakthrough, it will probably require a choice. I know. It stinks.

Second, the easiest thing to do is nothing. It would be easier to forget you found pornography or pretend like it never happened. Forgetting or pretending will be easier for a while but will it improve your relationship? Is living a lie the way you want to live?

Since we want change and doing nothing isn't our best option, let's embrace the questions. Let's make the hard choices.

God is willing to give you the guts to choose the hard, the courage to challenge the I'll nevers and the smarts to know Spanx are never a bad choice.

> Life is a matter of choices, and every choice you make makes you.
>
> —JOHN C. MAXWELL

A CALL TO COURAGE

It's Choice Day! Today is the day to make a choice you've been dreading or putting off. Not sure what decision needs to be made? Let's do a brain dump. Dumping your brain on paper leaves more mental space for routine things like the grocery list, eating, and feeding the dog.

Make a list of decisions that are on your plate. Dump them all out on paper. Do you need to decide on a counselor? Do you need to have a difficult conversation with your husband or someone else? Do you need to be tested for STDs? Do you have financial questions that need answers? Do you need to decide what to cook for supper? Make a list to clear up some mental space.

Next, take your list before the Lord. He knows there's a lot swirling around in your brain. Ask Him to show you your next step. Just ONE step. Not the next ten steps, but the choice you need to make today.

Then do it.

Chapter Five

WE'RE BETTER TOGETHER

Two are better than one,
  because they have a good return for their labor:
If either of them falls down,
  one can help the other up.
But pity anyone who falls
  and has no one to help them up.
Also, if two lie down together, they will keep warm.
  But how can one keep warm alone?
Ecclesiastes 4:9-11

It's not often we have friends for decades. Friends who have seen our Aqua Net saturated hair of the eighties, walked with us through final exams, boy troubles, poor style choices (parachute pants), and all sorts of things in between. If we're lucky, we have one or two friends who have been privy to a front row seat to our lives and us to theirs.

When my husband moved out that Saturday, I was an emotional wreck. I vacillated between grief and anger. I was annoyed, irritated, and a weepy mess. Even though I knew I had made the right decision, it was devastating for all of us.

I wept. I was lonely. And I knew I needed people in my life to walk this painful journey with me. I couldn't manage alone. Nor did I want to. That meant I needed to humble myself and reveal the less-than-perfect version of my marriage and family.

My emotions were too raw for a phone call. That left me in a puddle of tears which isn't bad, but I needed a break from crying. Email was a better option for me. I wasn't sleeping anyway, so I had plenty of time in the middle of the night.

For the first few days after Sam moved out my children slept with me. Finding out their dad had made bad choices shattered their hearts. Crisis calls for extra TLC. We would crawl into my bed, talk, cry, and pray. Then it was off to sleepy town for my little people. For me? Not so much.

Falling asleep was difficult between two wiggly kids and two weeping eyes. Eventually the sobs slowed to silent tears and the wiggles gave way to sleep, and I managed to fall asleep.

Inevitably I would wake up hours before the beeping of the alarm and quietly slip out of bed. On a good night I'd crash in one of my kids' bed and sleep until morning. On a not-so-good night, I'd be awake until the alarm went off.

Those dark and quiet hours in the middle of the night were long. My middle-of-the-night activities included panic, crying, and rehashing conversations and actions from months past. I also used those dark hours to communicate with friends.

The first night I sent an email to two longtime friends to let them know Sam had moved out. Jill and Susan are my Aqua Net friends, friends who signed long notes in my high school yearbooks, tolerated my need to never stop for directions, and shared multiple purple cans of the infamous hairspray. The three of us could finish off a quart of Rocky Road ice cream with three spoons and a movie. They are the friends who have loved me for decades.

I sent them an email early Sunday morning and by Tuesday they were standing on my doorstep. They lived three hours away and had their own families to manage but dropped everything just to be with me, to support me. They cried with me and for me.

And then there's Becky. We don't go as far back as the Aqua Net era, but I bet she used some Aqua Net back in the day. Our friendship started in our early married days, so we have done some life together. We've traveled the Southeast to hear Beth Moore speak, scrapbooked, and closed Outback after many hours of conversation.

Unfortunately, Becky lives a couple of hours away. Fortunately for us, she doesn't mind standing in line at the post office and is a generous gift-giver. For the first six months of my separation, she sent the kids and me numerous packages in the mail. I don't mean packages in pint-sized boxes but giant packages that included games, books, and home-made treats. We were always excited to see a package from her on our front porch. She and her packages were a bright spot.

But sometimes God brings people in our lives just in the nick of time. Just weeks before my husband moved out, I met Rene'. Her husband was coming on staff at our church, and I went to a meet and greet for them. Not sure how to explain it but somehow God connected our hearts and fast-tracked our friendship.

When my marriage crumbled weeks later, she was there to help me pick up the pieces. She was there to help me sort out the details. She was there to remind me what was true. She was there to play board games, listen to me cry, and remind me to take care of myself.

Do you have friends who have walked the distance with you? Friends who have seen you at your worst and love you anyway. People who change tires, fix headlights, play games, and love on your kids. Or people who listen, give great advice, and make good soup. Whoever they are, I hope you choose to invite them into your pain.

Then there are virtual friends, ones we have connected with on Facebook or Instagram or blogs with authors who seem like friends. And maybe even some genuine social media friends. Using discern-ment with who we trust on social media is always in order. It's easy to be swayed by well-meaning people who tell us what we want to hear.

A break from social media may be in order. I find that I need to check out from social media around holidays. Everybody's marriage looks perfect on Instagram. The kids are dressed in matching pajamas, the lighting is just right, and everybody looks happy behind their white-teethed smiles.

That might be too much for you to handle right now. Be kind to yourself and give yourself permission to take a break from social media for a while if that's what you need.

Because we are hurting and broken, we can be susceptible to people who might take advantage of our vulnerability. We always need to be wise in our choice of friends, but especially when we're hurting or emotional. One thing is for sure: We don't need to bear our souls and feelings to male friends or co-workers. Countless affairs have innocently started that way. Let's not assume we'll be the exception. We must guard our hearts, especially when they're broken.

The bottom line is we need people. Having the Body of Christ has been one of the largest avenues of the healing process for me. Do you have people in your life who can walk this road with you?

God was gracious to design us to do life with other people. For sure friendships can be sticky or hard sometimes. Jesus modeled a life with friends. When His life was hard, he didn't try to do it on His own. When He knew the cross was coming, He invited His friends to walk the road with Him. He went to the Garden of Gethsemane with three friends by His side. Three flawed and human friends. But friends, nonetheless.

> Then Jesus went with his disciples to a place called Gethsemane, and he said to them, "Sit here while I go over there and pray." He took Peter and the two sons of Zebedee along with him, and he began to be sorrowful and troubled. Then he said to them, "My soul is overwhelmed with sorrow to the point of death. Stay here and keep watch with me."
>
> *Matthew 26:36-38*

Are you overwhelmed with sorrow or feel like something is dying? Your marriage, your family, your dreams. Please don't try to sort out your situation and heartache on your own. I hope you'll invite people into your life to walk alongside you, to love on you, and to cry with you. Sure, some people can be difficult and unloving, but the Body of Christ is a sweet place to hang your hat. Hairspray and all.

> I get by with a little help from my friends.
>
> — THE BEATLES

A CALL TO COURAGE

Identify godly female friends who can walk this journey with you and steer you in a biblical direction. It may be a new friend God brings to you for this season or an old friend who steps back into your life for a period of time. Or a friend you connect with once a week or from a distance. One thing is certain—we are not meant to carry this burden alone. You might be pleasantly surprised who makes time for you. It's also helpful, and validating, to surround yourself with other women who are walking a similar journey.

A CALL TO COURAGE FOR FRIENDS

We have people in our lives who want to help us, but they have no idea how. We want to tell them how to help but our brain is too mushy to think of ideas. I have included a few ideas here. Add any others that would be helpful to you.

- Text you short prayers or verses.
- Commit to pray regularly for you.
- Pray with you on the phone or in person.
- Call or text to check on you, even if you don't have the emotional capacity to respond.
- Visit you.
- Bring you a meal.
- Listen to you cry or rehash the story one more time.
- Grocery shop.

- Take your children on an outing.
- Take you to lunch.
- Help you think through your choices.
- Help you make a clear list of the top two to four things you need to do in the next week and repeat.
- Give you genuine compliments.
- Gently help you see your reality.
- Help you brainstorm/problem solve different areas (relationships, finances, parenting).
- Help with research on different topics (finding a counselor, helping children walk through hard things, housing, books to read).
- Remind you to take time to replenish yourself.
- Give you a movie ticket, pedicure, etc. to remind you to replenish yourself. Some people really want to do this.
- Encourage you through notes or gifts in the mail.
- Remind you that God is bigger than your problem.
- Don't dismiss your pain and heartbreak.
- Don't let you wallow in depression and anxiety without getting help.
- Love on your children.
- Praise your efforts.
- Remind you of what *is* true, not what seems true.
- Pick up your children from school.
- Help your children with homework.
- Don't give up on you.
- Remind you that you're normal.

Chapter Six

NO SHAME ON ME

> Now the Lord is the Spirit, and where the Spirit of the Lord is, there is freedom.
> *2 Corinthians 3:17*

You may be okay in the friend department. Perhaps you have shared a can of Aqua Net or deep secrets with friends who know your gripes, fears, and pant size. But this subject, your husband's pornography use, has you tongue-tied when it comes to sharing your struggle with friends. Something about it seems harder, more shameful.

That was the case with me. Telling even the dearest of friends that my husband had an issue with pornography felt awkward and embarrassing. Just saying those words stirred up a profound sense of humiliation. Deep down it made it seem like there was something wrong with me.

For years I told myself I was protecting my husband's reputation by not telling friends or the girls in Bible study. My self-righteousness told me I was protecting God's image by not letting people know about our struggles. When, in fact, I was protecting my reputation and my image.

The reality of my marriage would tarnish the Christian, church-going girl image that had taken a lifetime to build. If I could maintain the facade of a perfect marriage, maybe it would morph into the marriage I had always dreamed of. So, I kept silent.

Admitting our husband's pornography use is embarrassing, especially in the church world. We're supposed to have it all together, right? Sam and I looked like a happy couple. Why would I want to shatter that perception?

The self-imposed silence I experienced is the same silence that keeps men enslaved to pornography. That silence has a name. Shame. And shame kept my mouth closed.

Shame can trick us into believing silence is the best way forward. Because shame feels dishonorable, we keep quiet. None of us church-going girls want to be perceived as dishonorable, so silence seems like a better option.

The enemy is far from all-knowing, but he knows that much. Satan lures men into pornography and controls through shame. He does the same with us. It's a two-for-one for the enemy. When men and women suffer in silence the only one winning is the enemy.

Admitting the reality of my marriage was the beginning of the journey of breaking free from shame. I had to face the fact that my marriage was a mess. Pretending or ignoring was no longer an option nor did it help.

When I took time to dig into why I was too ashamed to tell someone, I realized I was experiencing an inconsistency between my values and my reality. I valued marriage based on biblical principles with open communication and a healthy sexual relationship. I valued friendship and togetherness. What I was living was far from that.

We were two strangers receiving mail at the same house. There was no cultivating a friendship or having meaningful conversations. Physical intimacy was a thing of the past. We were going through the motions while offering the world outside our house something that wasn't happening inside our house. We were trying to "fake it till you make it."

Fake it till you make it may work for some people, but not for me. It feels too inauthentic. Sure, we need to muscle through certain things, but fake it till you make it isn't my go-to life mantra. It's pretending your life is something it's not. Everything about that screams, well, fake.

Do you feel fake? It's possible you're struggling because your reality doesn't match your values. You feel conflicted and inconsistent because the two don't line up. When we know there is a lack of consistency in our lives, we can feel like a fraud. When we don't feel honest, it's easier to feel judged by other people.

Judging is forming an opinion about someone or something. We all make judgements. I've done that more times than I can count. I remember attending a women's retreat several years ago. At our first group meeting, I noticed a striking lady off to the side of the conference room. She was attractive with great skin, beautiful hair, and an outgoing personality. I immediately sized her up in my mind as perfect.

Later in the retreat, I wasn't surprised to find she was on the program for one of the sessions. I sighed. Here we go again. Another beautiful person telling us regular people how to live. But I was surprised, and humbled, when I heard her story. She had been homeless. That was a wakeup call to my judgmental heart.

Judgmental hearts are the same reason the "woman at the well" chose not to draw water in the cool hours of the morning. In John 4, the Bible tells us about a shame-filled woman who waited until the middle of the day to draw water at the well, and it wasn't because she was a late sleeper. She knew if she waited until the scorching sun was high in the sky the more respectable women wouldn't be there, and she would avoid their judgmental eyes. This woman had been through five husbands. Her current man was not her husband. She was a woman with a poor reputation and a track record to prove it.

But Jesus doesn't care about track records or reputations. He cares about redemption. On this midday visit to the well, she ran into Jesus. She may have gone for water, but Jesus had come for her. Her surprise encounter with Jesus did the same thing for her that it does for us, it changed her.

She left her shame at the well and told the town about Jesus. Many in the town believed in Jesus because of her testimony.

Like the woman at the well, we can leave our shame behind and present the people in our lives with an opportunity, an opportunity to love like Christ. When we expose the reality of our marriage, we take our circumstances and place them in the hands of others. Giving them a choice. Will they choose to accept us or judge us?

Putting your reality out there for the world to see is hard, even for the strongest person. Nobody wants to be judged based on someone else's actions.

Let's not underestimate people. Sure, there will be those who look down on us or criticize us. There will also be plenty of people who will hurt alongside us. Pornography in the church is prevalent, even if it's not obvious. You may be surprised who identifies with your pain.

You know what I found to be true about the people in my life? Maybe it's also true about the people in your life. They are far less judgmental than I thought. People locked arms with my family and fought the battle with us.

That is what it has been. A battle.

Oh, if life only played out like a Hallmark movie where everybody looks beautiful, the girl always gets the guy, and it's wrapped up in a neat bow in two hours. But since the Hallmark way isn't God's way, I'm relieved to know we are equipped with the finest of weapons for our battle. Weapons money can't buy and this earth can't provide.

God unveils our arsenal of weapons in Ephesians 6—the armor of God. These weapons are available to those who are followers of Christ. God wouldn't have given us armor if we weren't in a battle.

When I look over the list of armor, the shield of faith catches my attention. The Roman shield was the shape of a rectangle and about the size of a small door. Soldiers used their shield to deflect flaming arrows from the enemy. Yes, it was carefully crafted and maintained to ensure the soldier was protected during battle, but how soldiers used it makes it fascinating.

When the soldiers advanced toward an enemy wall, the soldiers gathered in a tight formation. The front row held their shields out in front while the soldiers in the middle and back held their shields overhead. This linking of shields formed a turtle-like shell. This tactic not only protected the soldiers individually but collectively to give them quite the advantage.

When shame keeps us from inviting people into our pain, we are left fighting our battle alone. We are left holding our shield without the covering of a fellow soldier. We are sure to have days when we're too exhausted or weepy to even pick it up. We desperately need fellow shield holders.

Trying to shield ourselves from embarrassment by keeping quiet leaves us to fight alone. The battle is too long and too hard to go at it without people in our corner. Let's not let shame decide who our fighting friends are.

> Shame erodes our courage and fuels disengagement.
>
> — BRENÉ BROWN

A CALL TO COURAGE

Do you feel the fiery arrows of shame and embarrassment flying your way? Do you feel completely humiliated? Maybe you're telling yourself "I can handle it on my own" as a way to avoid telling someone what's going on.

Ask God to bring to mind one trusted person with whom to share your story. Just one. Maybe it's a friend from your list or a trusted pastor, sister, counselor, or aunt. Share your story. Give someone the opportunity to choose to love like Christ.

I assure you of two things: it will be hard, and it will be freeing. You can do it. You may find it easier to write out your story and read it to them. Whatever works for you. No need to suffer in silence a day longer.

Sometimes people mean well in the advice they give. If someone tells you it's your fault, don't listen to them. Well-meaning people who love us sometimes offer terrible advice because they have no idea what they're talking about.

Chapter Seven

NOT WHAT I EXPECTED

In the morning, LORD, you hear my voice;
  in the morning I lay my requests before you
  and wait expectantly.
Psalm 5:3

While I rushed around the house getting ready for a class at church, I realized I needed money for food. Sam is a keeper of all things, so I knew he'd have a stash of loose change. I rummaged through his nightstand looking for money. I did find change. But I also found adult videos that had been checked out from a video store far from our house.

My heart sank. Again. This marked the second time I discovered pornography, only months after the first discovery.

Since our neighbor was waiting for me, I crammed the videos back into the drawer and scratched around to find the money I needed. I didn't take time to process my discovery or dare mention it to my neighbor.

I must have gone to church acting like nothing happened. I can't remember. I do remember the sense of urgency to race home to return the videos.

This time my reaction to finding pornography wasn't near as gracious. Sure, my heart was broken but my blood was boiling. After the first discovery I expected things to be different. I expected there to be no pornography. Once we expect something to be different, failure to meet expectations is difficult to swallow.

We all have expectations. We expect water to gush from a faucet. We expect a blast of cold air when we open the refrigerator. We expect the sun to rise every morning. And it's reasonable to expect no pornography in our relationship.

Sam and I worked through the second pornography discovery. We went to counseling and set aside time for date nights. We eventually moved to a new house in a different city. I hoped the move would be the fresh start we needed.

As the months passed, so did the excitement of a new house. The freshly painted walls and neighbors were new, but the heartache was the same. Sam and I did enjoy times of connectedness and laughter, but we mostly lived like roommates. We presented a united front to our children, Bennett and Grace, and the rest of the world. We looked good from the outside.

A lot of families look good from the outside. A scroll through social media shows families taking road trips complete with flawless pictures. Families wearing matching Christmas pajamas. Families with all the friends, all the stuff, and all the fun. Families like yours and mine who long for their reality to match what they post on social media.

I'm not suggesting all social media posts are a lie. There are plenty of great trips, moments of closeness, and beautiful memories. But sometimes when the cameras are turned off, the bickering turns on, or the silent treatment, sarcasm, or emotional distance.

The distance between reality and Instagram posts can be a depressing chasm, one fueled by inconsistency. The life we're living isn't the life we want to live.

In chapter six, I wrote about how we feel shame when our reality doesn't match our values. What happens when our reality doesn't match our expectations? When what we expected doesn't match what is happening, our unmet expectations can lead to disappointment.

I imagine you're feeling disappointed because what you expected isn't happening. What once was is no longer. The marriage you thought you'd have when you said, "I do" has turned into, "I'd rather not."

When my prayers weren't answered the way I thought they should be and life wasn't going the way I expected, disappointment replaced expectation. I was disappointed with Sam and myself. And, if I'm gut-level honest, I was disappointed with God.

God has the power to do anything. His power can change hearts and raise people from the dead. I just needed Him to change our hearts and raise our dead marriage. But He didn't.

Until Jesus returns, disappointments, big and small, will be part of our lives. Someone will forget our birthday. We'll feel left out. On a day we really want ice cream, the ice cream machine at McDonald's will be broken.

When what we had planned in our minds doesn't pan out in our lives, the result is disappointment. Make no mistake, God has a plan. It may not be our plan, but He's not wringing his hands wondering what to do next. And no plan of the Lord can be thwarted even if we expected something different.

When we expect certain outcomes and even pray to that end, we limit our future to our imagination or our way of thinking. Expectation gives us tunnel vision for a fixed outcome without the flexibility for God to do something, well, unexpected. God, the Maker of the Northern Lights, rainbows, and laughter, has a bigger, better plan that our human minds can conjure up.

I'm not saying we shouldn't tell Him our desires and pray with boldness. Do I think you should pray for God to save your marriage? Absolutely. Do I think we should pray for specifics for ourselves, our children, and others? Of course. But when we hold tightly to what we think is best, our hands are closed to what God might be trying to give us.

It would be nice if God explained what His plans for us are. It would be nice, but it wouldn't be faith. If he spelled it out for us, we wouldn't need faith. We are called to live by faith and not by sight.

The Israelites lived every day in the wilderness with a visible glimpse of God. They truly walked by sight. They saw the cloud that covered them and led them by day. They experienced the fire that gave them light at night. They saw God's manifest presence, yet they still grumbled and complained. And they were disappointed their trip to the Promised Land wasn't going the way they expected.

Remember the story of Jonah? He was the poster child for being disappointed with God. When God asked Jonah to preach to the Ninevites, he bolted it in the opposite direction instead. But God got his attention through an unrelenting storm and a stint inside the belly of a big fish. When Jonah finally came to his senses and obeyed God, he was disappointed with the outcome. God showed compassion on the people of Nineveh and Jonah didn't like it one bit.

But the story of Jonah ends abruptly. The Bible doesn't say that Jonah came around and finally saw things God's way. We have no idea what happened to Jonah. The last chapter of Jonah ends with no resolution. No indication that Jonah changed his attitude or that he died. Nothing.

In Jonah 4:10-11, we read: "But the LORD said, 'You have been concerned about this plant, though you did not tend it or make it grow. It sprang up overnight and died overnight. And should I not have concern for the great city of Nineveh, in which there are more than a hundred and twenty thousand people who cannot tell their right hand from their left—and also many animals?'"

The last words penned in the book of Jonah are a question, a question about Jonah's misplaced priorities. Jonah was concerned about the health of a plant, but God was concerned about the hearts of people.

Our priorities may not be misplaced but they may be different than God's priorities. He sees the whole wide world. We only see our little corner of the world. When two people have different perspectives, different priorities are inevitable often followed by disappointment.

When you feel disappointed with God, you may find it helpful to work through these steps:

1. We must admit it.

Get it out in the open and tell God you're disappointed He didn't do what you hoped He would. You don't have to pretend or hide your disappointment from Him. Be honest. He already knows. You need not sugar coat it or minimize it or Christianize it to make it sound spiritual. Just tell Him.

1 Timothy 1:5 says, "But the goal of our instruction is love from a pure heart, from a good conscience, and from a sincere faith." If we want to have deep faith that crosses decades and generations, we must have a sincere faith—an authentic relationship with Jesus that is solid enough to be honest about our joys, heartaches, and disappointments.

2. Be honest with yourself too.

Admitting we're disappointed with God doesn't make us less of a Christian. It makes us genuine in our faith. Honesty is always the best policy. It takes courage, makes for healthier relationships, and shows emotional maturity.

3. Accept and process.

Once we've been honest with God and ourselves, we can do the work of accepting and processing our disappointment. We can let go of what we think God should do in our lives and open our eyes to what He is doing in our lives. For me, I was disappointed in how God answered my prayer for a breakthrough, but I was pleased that He was listening and moving in my life.

It's exciting to see God work in our lives. It's just not always easy or the way we would like it to be. Kay Arthur, author of *As Silver Refined: Learning to Embrace Life's Disappointments*, explains how God uses our disappointments: "The disappointment has come—not because God desires to hurt you or make you miserable or to demoralize you or ruin your life or keep you from ever knowing happiness. He wants you to be perfect and complete in every aspect, lacking nothing. It's not the easy times that make you more like Jesus, but the hard times."

That's the end game, to be like Jesus. God is using our disappointments to make us more like Him. I'm just glad he's not using the belly of a fish.

> When you release expectations, you are free to enjoy things for what they are instead of what you think they should be.
>
> — MANDY HALE

A CALL TO COURAGE

What step are you on? Having genuine faith and pursuing an authentic relationship with Jesus isn't for sissies. Get honest with God about your disappointments.

Chapter Eight

STAY IN THE WORD

> For the word of God is alive and active. Sharper than any double-edged sword, it penetrates even to dividing soul and spirit, joints and marrow; it judges the thoughts and attitudes of the heart.
> *Hebrews 4:12*

After the discovery on that September Saturday, I was distraught and looking for guidance, desperate for anything that could help me make sense of the senseless. After the phone call to Sam, I made two other phone calls, one to a pastor and the other to my aunt. The advice I received from my pastor carried me for months. I share that same wisdom with other women who are walking this road or any difficult road. His simple but freeing advice was: Take one day at a time and stay in The Word.

I've never been a take-one-day-at-a-time kind of girl. I'm a planner constantly looking to the next thing. I used to rarely take one day at a time or make the most of the now. I've missed a lot of life by not living in the moment. Forward thinking isn't bad, it just needs to be balanced with living in the present.

Being emotionally distraught forced me to take one day at a time. When my husband moved out, thinking about more than one day overwhelmed me. I had no idea what the future held. Too much uncertainty made planning difficult. Just getting my kids to school without falling to pieces felt like success.

Being encouraged to live one day at a time was a huge relief, as if someone had given me permission to live life in the here and now. How many times have we been on vacation and been distracted by trying to get the perfect picture that we missed experiencing the moment? Living one day at a time was freedom to enjoy the moment and hope you get a good enough picture to slap in a scrapbook when you retire.

The second piece of advice proved to be the most life-giving. Stay in The Word. I've always been a Bible study girl. I have stacks of Bible study workbooks from the last twenty years. Getting together with other women and talking through The Word builds my faith. Now the time had come to put the years spent in Bible study to the test. Time to see if time in The Word makes a difference when hard times come. Is His Word really all it has claimed to be?

The answer is yes. An emphatic yes. The Bible is true, stands forever, and is the Good News our broken world and broken hearts need. God's Word has proven to be an anchor during tough times, salve for my wounded heart, and light for a journey I had no desire to take. I believe His Word can be that for your journey as well.

You may think this is a bit weird but there were plenty of nights I went to bed with my Bible laid wide open in the space where my husband should have been. I have no idea if osmosis is real, but it was my version of spiritual osmosis. I wanted anything and everything God had to offer, I yearned for every ounce of healing He was willing to give me.

I didn't just need the healing His Word offered. I needed hope, hope in a God who does outrageous things. In the Bible, this mysterious but life-giving book, God made a donkey talk, breathed life into dead people, and made the sun stand still in sky. He won battles with clay pots and unlikely warriors. He fed thousands with only a plateful of food. These very things, the unusual things of the Bible, brought me hope. If He can cause a storm to stop or turn water into blood, He can cause my heartache to stop and turn my chaos into calm.

Besides giving us healing and hope, His Word can also equip us to fight battles we never saw coming. God calls His Word the Sword of the Spirit. To us, swords are archaic symbols of honor and authority. God's Word is more than a symbol of victory. His Word is our means to victory.

Your victory may look different that my victory, but God's Word has the miraculous inexplicable ability to transform our lives and renew our thinking. That would be a victory for both of us.

So, let's pick up our swords and fight. Wield The Word like it has power to save lives, marriages, and families. Our life, marriage, and family. We might not have the emotional capacity to strike up a new discipline. These ideas are to consider, not a list to conquer.

- Pray The Word (take a look at chapter 3).
- Read the Bible out loud (Psalms is a great place to start.).
- Study the Bible (specific words, characters).
- Listen to biblically sound podcasts while getting ready for or driving to work.
- Listen to worship music.
- Listen to someone read the Bible.
- Go to Bible study.
- Go to a Bible-believing church.
- Paint, draw, color The Word.
- Grab a journaling Bible and bring The Word to color right inside your Bible.
- Memorize one verse. Just one.
- Meditate on one verse. Could be the same one you memorized.
- Write The Word.

You might be drained from the fight already. Weary from trying to make it all work. You feel like giving up, like it's not worth the effort.

It's possible you've lived your whole life with no one to fight for you. Your parents may have been busy fighting their own pain to help you navigate your life. Growing up you felt like you were on your own. There was no teacher or coach in your corner to cheer you on. And here you are married to the man who was supposed to fight for you but now you're fighting each other.

There is good news for exhausted girls like us. First, a nap is a good idea. I'm not kidding. When you're tired from the battle, rest. Give yourself permission to take a nap. You will find me most Sunday afternoons napping on my couch. A nap can increase alertness and creativity, reduce stress, boost memory, and brighten our mood.

There is a reason God rested on the seventh day of creation. Not because He needed rest, but because we do. He was modeling a healthy way to live.

Here is the second bit of good news. Moses told the Israelites in Exodus 14:14: "The Lord will fight for you; you need only to be still." God can do the same for you. Just like He fought for the Israelites, He will fight for you. When you can't muster the strength to wield your sword, God will fight for you.

What does it look like for God to fight for us? He can change another person's heart, change circumstances, or take away an impossible situation. He can give us wisdom for the next step or put people in our path to help us get to the next step. He can give us peace when peace seems unobtainable. Even when we don't recognize it, God is fighting for us. He is always working on our behalf.

While God fights for us, the enemy fights against us. Satan is giving his best effort to destroy our lives. And he's sneaky. He can twist words and string together sentences and ideas and make them seem true. He manipulates God's words to cause us to doubt Him. He did that to Eve in the Garden of Eden.

God's Word is the place we can go to rat out the enemy and his lies. When we stay in The Word, we are constantly immersed in truth equipping us to recognize the enemy's deception. His Word reminds us of what is true about us. Let me name a few:

But you are a **chosen people**, a royal priesthood, a holy nation, God's special possession, that you may declare the praises of him who called you out of darkness into his wonderful light.
1 Peter 2:9

See what great love the Father has lavished on us,
that we should be called **children of God**!
And that is what we are!
The reason the world does not know us
is that it did not know him.
1 John 3:1

For we are **God's handiwork**, created in Christ Jesus to do good works, which God prepared in advance for us to do.
Ephesians 2:10

I no longer call you servants because a servant does not know his master's business. Instead, **I have called you friends**, for everything that I learned from my Father I have made known to you.
John 15:15

No, in all these things we are **more than conquerors**
through him who loved us.
Romans 8:37

Therefore, as God's chosen people, holy and **dearly loved**,
clothe yourselves with compassion, kindness, humility,
gentleness, and patience.
Colossians 3:12

I imagine you aren't feeling like a conqueror today. You may not feel chosen or dearly loved. But God's Word says you are. He loves us and chooses us, even on the days we mess up terribly or we're a blubbering mess. Especially on those days, His Word is our source of truth assuring us of His affection for us and reminding us it's okay to take one day at a time.

The best thing about the future is that it comes one day at a time.

— ABRAHAM LINCOLN

A CALL TO COURAGE

A simple way to keep your mind focused on God's Word is to set a verse as the wallpaper on your phone or laptop. So, every time you click on your phone, or open your laptop, you will fill your mind with the truth of God's Word. Here are some Scripture suggestions:

God is our refuge and strength,
a very present help in trouble.
Psalm 46:1

Trust in the LORD with all your heart
and lean not on your own understanding;
in all your ways submit to him,
and he will make your paths straight.
Proverbs 3:5-6

The LORD is my shepherd, I lack nothing.
He makes me lie down in green pastures,
he leads me beside quiet waters, he refreshes my soul.
He guides me along the right paths
for his name's sake.
Psalm 23:1-3

Chapter Nine

HE KNOWS

"For I know the plans I have for you," declares the
LORD, "plans to prosper you and not to harm you,
plans to give you hope and a future."
Jeremiah 29:11

During the first few weeks of my separation, life was a blur. I spent a lot of time crying. Sleeping was a struggle. I'd fall asleep only to wake up a couple of hours later, long before the sun came up. And eating seemed completely unnecessary. A little peanut butter and chocolate for lunch seemed like a fine meal at the time.

While I muddled from one day to the next, an endless list of questions rolled around my brain. Questions that haunted me when the nights wouldn't end. Questions that occupied my days when I tried to remember to pick up my kids. Then there were questions from dear friends who were helping me sort out life. So many questions begging for answers.

I'm guessing you have your share of questions begging for answers too. What are your questions? Mine included: What have I done? Am

I okay? Are my children okay? What's next? What about our finances?

Your questions may be different than mine, but we may have similar answers. As I wrestled for answers only one answer came to mind. One honest-to-the-bone answer:

I don't know.

I muttered I don't know over and over. I shrugged and shook my head with the only honest answer I could muster. I don't know. I didn't know what to do next. I didn't know how to help my kids through the pain. I was at a loss for answers.

You may be at a loss for answers too, with no idea how to navigate your new life. Do you call a counselor, tell somebody what's happening, or do you just take a nap? I recommend all three.

Not knowing is a rough place to be. A bit helpless and unfamiliar even. We live in a world where knowledge is at our fingertips, thanks to Google. In the blink of an eye, we can find out what's on a menu, the price of a pair of shoes, how people rated a potential purchase, and, of great importance, if TJ Maxx is open.

While I'm personally thankful for knowledge at the swipe of a finger, Google falls short when it comes to knowing what the future holds. There is only One who knows what choices will be made, the intentions of another, and what obstacles and blessings await us.

He also knows how many hairs are left on our aging, but beautiful, heads. He knows how many stars light up the sky each night. He knows our sins, our secrets, and a host of other things we only memorized for the test. He knows even if we don't.

I confess that I like knowing things. It's nice to be the person who wins in Trivial Pursuit and the person who finds the destination without directions. Most people I know enjoy being 'in the know.'

But what happens when our lingering answer to life's questions leaves us out of the know? We find ourselves in the chasm between wanting to know yet not knowing. We want answers but they're painfully absent.

The lack of answers reminds us that we're not in the driver's seat, causing us to scramble for anything that makes sense. Yes, we absolutely need to educate ourselves. Yes, making wise choices is necessary.

Yes, to setting boundaries. And yes, to taking care of ourselves. These things can help bring clarity and much-needed answers, but sometimes we can't research our way into an answer.

After our fretting is done, which may happen numerous times a day, day after day, we are still left with unknowns. When we've clambered our way into exhaustion or taken all the wise steps we can think of, we are still left with an uncertain future and unanswered questions.

When we don't have all the answers, our only action is to trust. You and I can bridge the gap between knowing and not knowing by trusting in a God who has no limit to what He knows. He knows things we don't know to ask. And because He knows what our future holds, we can trust Him to hold it.

Since God is the Great Knower, He may lead us in ways and to places we may not have chosen ourselves. I'm not suggesting God intentionally led us to where we are. I'm saying we probably wouldn't have chosen our circumstances any more than we would have chosen dental surgery.

Just like we didn't choose our circumstances, Mary, the mother of Jesus, didn't choose to be a teenage mom. Noah wouldn't have chosen to the be the crazy guy building an ark with no rain on the horizon. The disciples wouldn't have chosen to be on a stormy sea, the leper wouldn't have chosen his healing to come from a muddy river, and the blind man may not have chosen spit as his healing ointment.

But God knew what was on the other side.

In Exodus we read the story of God moving His people, the Israelites, from Egypt to the land He had promised them. A land where they would no longer live as slaves. Moses was God's man to lead His people to the new land. After Moses petitioned Pharaoh several times to let the Israelites go, Pharaoh finally agreed after numerous supernatural happenings. And their journey began.

Moses left Egypt with a multitude of Israelites in tow on a journey they never would have taken had they known the future. The road God led them on might not have been the road they would have taken. But God knew the future.

When Pharaoh let the people go God did not lead them on the

road through the Philistine country, though that was shorter. For God said, "If they face war, they might change their minds and return to Egypt." So God led the people around by the desert road toward the Red Sea. The Israelites went up out of Egypt ready for battle. (See Exodus 13:17-18.)

God intentionally led them the longer, desert way toward the Red Sea instead of the shorter way. What? The long way? To my efficient get-it-done mind that seems wrong. But the long way it was.

If you're not familiar with the story, Pharaoh eventually regretted his decision of letting the Israelites go. So, Pharaoh gathered his army and pursued the Israelites. The Israelites found themselves stuck in quite the predicament. They were stuck between the Red Sea, where God intentionally led them, and the Egyptian army. Both directions looked like death. Unless you're God.

What God did next defied gravity. Literally.

God caused a strong wind to blow all night that divided the water of the Red Sea. He created a path between two walls of water giving the Israelites a way of escape from the pursuing Egyptians.

Having heard this story since I was a kid, wonder has taken a back-seat to familiarity. As I think about it now, it seems a strong wind blowing all night piling up water would be a bit on the scary side. Maybe it's just me.

Then, as you got up the next morning, if you managed any sleep at all, you approach the Red Sea to see two walls of water with a path between them. I would have thought, "You mean, that's the plan? You want me to take my family, everything I own and walk between two walls of water held up only by wind? Surely there is a Plan B."

Nope. No Plan B. Walking through a wall of water on each side was the actual plan—a plan that sounded pretty outrageous and downright scary. It would take some kind of courage and faith for me to step my size eleven foot onto the dry ground between the water. But that's what the Israelites did. They tightened the laces on their sandals, grabbed their stuff, and stepped onto the dry ground God had miraculously created for them.

If you don't know the story, they did make it through. I can't say the same for the Egyptian army. They tried to catch the Israelites but drowned. The miracle was only meant for God's people.

If God had not taken His people the on longer, harder road, they would have never experienced the miracle of Him parting the Red Sea.

For whatever reason God has allowed this leg of our journey to be hard, scary even. Only He knows why we are on this road. He knows what will happen tomorrow, next week, and next year. It's possible this hard road may be leading us straight into a miracle—one we wouldn't experience any other way.

If you're like me, you'd rather not be in a position to need a miracle. You probably don't need a body of water parted but you could use the miracle of financial provision or a new job or a changed heart. Or all those things. You may have no idea what miracle you need. The good news is, we don't have to know what we need for God to give it to us. We don't have to know the answers. We just keep putting one foot in front of the other, one day at a time.

When your nights are long, your brain is foggy, and you just don't know, you can find hope in knowing the One who knows it all. As you muddle through your days with "I don't know" falling from your lips, be encouraged. We can trust God with our unknowns. They are not unknown to Him.

> Never be afraid to trust an unknown future to a known God.
>
> — CORRIE TEN BOOM

A CALL TO COURAGE

Life is swimming with uncertainties. Make a list of all the things that are up in the air or you're unsure of. You might start with your relationship, finances, and living situation.

Your list might be long and exhaustive. That's okay. It's safe to acknowledge our humanness—to admit we're clueless about what to do next, what to say, or how to act. Thank God for knowing every detail of your life, past, present, and future.

Remind Him of the miracle He did for the Israelites at the Red Sea and be bold enough to ask Him for your miracle.

Chapter Ten

MEDICINE AND SALT

"Come to me, all you who are weary and burdened, and I will give you rest."
Matthew 11:28

When my children were preschoolers, I joined a Bible study at the church where they attended. I can't remember the name of the Bible study, but I do remember the name of the friend I met there, Jenn.

More than a decade has passed and we're still friends. It's refreshing to have friends who are honest but gracious. I'm thankful for godly friends who speak the truth even when you don't know you need to hear it. That's Jenn.

During the preschool years, my marriage hit an all-time low. Frustration was evident on both sides. If I had to pinpoint a time I noticed a change in our marriage, it would be the preschool years. We both had changed.

Change is inevitable and even necessary when you have children. While things were strained, I do remember times we laid on our faces praying together.

Pornography lurked in the background. I just didn't know it. I'm not sure when a bad habit becomes an addiction, but things were headed in that direction.

While Sam was secretly struggling with pornography, I was struggling with Dr. Jekyll, Mr. Hyde Syndrome. I don't think that's an actual medical term, but it was the right description of my symptoms. Maybe you've had it too. I could be happy one minute but sobbing fifteen minutes later. Then give me twenty more minutes and I'd be so angry I couldn't see straight. My feet felt like ice cubes. A good night's sleep was a thing of the past, and I looked like it. I was a mess. And it wasn't PMS.

Sometime during the emotional roller coaster ride of Dr. Jekyll, Mr. Hyde Syndrome, and after spending $3,000 on a mattress, I remember having a conversation on the phone with Jenn. I sat on my new mattress lamenting the state of my marriage. I was contemplating giving up. I was done. I was over living in a loveless marriage. This was it. When Sam got home from his work trip, I was leaving. I'd just pack up my kids and go to a hotel. I'm not sure why I thought raising two preschoolers as a single (unemployed) mom sounded easier but, at the time, it did.

This was one of those times when having a godly friend who was willing to speak truth into my life mattered. Jenn said, "Jody, listen to yourself. You're not making any sense. This is not who you are or who you want to be. This is not what you want for your family. Maybe there's something wrong. You should go to the doctor."

She was right. That was not me. I did want to fight for my marriage and my family. I did want to leave a legacy of love and commitment for my children. So, I went to the doctor. He diagnosed me with hypothyroidism. What a relief! Finally, a name to this unknown life-altering condition. I was finally able to get back on a less emotional, more stable track. And I was finally able to sleep. Thank goodness for medication.

And thank goodness for good friends. I hope you have a friend in your life that has permission to remind you who you are and call you out when you're not acting like yourself or the person you want to be. A friend who helps you take care of yourself even when you don't know you need it.

When my hypothyroidism was managed, I assumed my marriage would improve. Maybe it did for a while, but the underlying issues were still lurking in the dark and growing darker. Not just the pornography but the dark cloud that had settled over me. Joy had been sucked out of my life. Back to the doctor for me. Because of all the emotional turmoil and whatever else was rolling around my mind, the doctor diagnosed with me depression. What? I'm a happy person. He suggested medication. At first, I was resistant. My pride told me I'd be fine. My gut told me otherwise.

The doctor explained it like this: "Medicine is like salt. Sometimes we need salt to make our food taste better and sometimes we need medicine to make our lives better." That was true for my hypothyroidism diagnosis. Thyroid medicine had made my life better. Time for more salt.

Fortunately, my depression was situational and my need for medicine temporary. That's not always the case. Sometimes anxiety, depression, or other emotionally debilitating conditions are a daily struggle for an extended period or a lifetime. We may need medication to get us through a season or to get us through our lives.

Years later when I was muddling through separation and eventually divorce, nighttime pondering kept me awake. I would fall asleep only to wake up a few hours later and stare at the ceiling most of the night. My brain wouldn't shut off. I could spend three hours solving the traffic flow problem in the church parking lot and brainstorm how Walmart checkout could be more efficient if they'd just open one of the 25 lanes.

Besides the inefficient checkout system, I had plenty to think about. Thoughts of ripping the last thread of the security rug out from underneath my children overwhelmed me. I had no idea how I would survive financially. Could I manage life as a single mom? I mulled over the past and worried about the future.

You may find yourself rolling situations around in your mind over and over or dwelling on the same thoughts. Or paralyzed when making decisions by analyzing every detail.

Overthinking is defined as spending more time thinking about something than is necessary or productive. Are you struggling with the endless loop of overthinking by rehashing past conversations or focusing on problems? You're not alone in your thought loop.

Yes, we need to research and consider our options when making decisions. We need to be aware of how we manage conversations. But if our reflecting and research is affecting our daily lives or causing us to lose sleep, we may have a case of overthinking.

Overthinking is certainly understandable. A walk down the peanut butter aisle at the grocery store is enough to exhaust our decision-making skills. There are forty different kinds of peanut butter. Who knew you could crush and serve a peanut so many ways?

The average person makes 35,000 decisions every day. How many times to hit the snooze button. What mascara to use. Skirt or jeans. Cereal or toast. Smooth or crunchy. With so many decisions begging for answers, no wonder we suffer from overthinking.

Overthinking ushers in an avalanche of thoughts and paves the road to anxiety. If we can rein in our thoughts, we might experience less anxiety. We don't have to be held captive by our thoughts. We can hold our thoughts captive. (See 2 Corinthians 10:5.)

We get to be the boss of our thoughts. We get to decide what we think and when we think it.

How do we take thoughts captive? Self-awareness is half the battle. Paying attention to our thoughts is the first step to overcoming overthinking. We will need to be mindful and catch ourselves thinking unhealthy or obsessive thoughts, or thoughts we don't need to be thinking at that time. Then intentionally choose to think something else. We can't just tell ourselves to stop thinking something, we need to replace the thought with another thought. It takes practice, effort, and time, but it can happen. Yes, for you.

When I find myself thinking an unhealthy thought, I picture myself worshiping God at His feet in front of His throne. That gets my mind off the thought and puts my focus on Him. That is working for me these days. When it stops working, I'll try something else. It's an intentional distraction. Your distraction could be scripture, a declaration, worship, or a visual of some kind that pulls you out of the thought loop. You can never go wrong with meditating on or memorizing scripture.

Whatever you choose as your distraction, know that you are capable of winning the battle for your mind. Satan is a loser. You are a winner.

Before I knew about stopping the thought loop, I didn't feel like a winner. I mainly felt sleepy. I didn't know that a wacky sleep pattern was a sign of anxiety. A friend insisted I take another trip to the doctor and try medication one more time. "What do you have to lose?" she asked. She was right. I needed a little more salt for my journey. Taking medicine for a few months during our separation was one of the kindest things I did for myself.

Taking medication isn't a cure all or for all. Not all sleeplessness or symptoms require medicine. That is for a trusted doctor to decide.

Some people may see taking medicine for anxiety or depression as weakness. We are all allowed to have an opinion. That doesn't make one right and one wrong. Just different. I choose to see it as strength. To have the wherewithal to recognize a need and be willing to do something about it sounds like a strength. I agree that medicine can be a crutch when we don't want to do the work to be emotionally well, but that's a discussion for a different book.

If you struggle with anxiety or depression, be assured you are not alone. For whatever reason, Christians are expected to be immune to anxiety and depression. If we just loved God more or prayed more or read our Bible more, then we'd be free from depression. David might say otherwise. In Psalm 6 David freely expresses his depression to the Lord yet God still called him a man after His own heart.

It seems we have adopted Bob Marley's mantra as our Christian refrain, "Don't worry. Be happy." That sounds like a great way of life, until it isn't. It's good in theory but not in reality. People struggle. Jesus wouldn't address these issues if people didn't. Anxiety and depression are not Christian/non-Christian issues. They are human problems that affect millions of people every single day.

If you're one of those people, take comfort knowing that "The Lord is close to the brokenhearted and saves those who are crushed in spirit" (Psalm 34:18).

When you're feeling crushed in spirit, pray, read your Bible, and take your thoughts captive. Allow trusted friends to speak into your life. And take care of yourself, the outside and the inside. But remember, if you feel depressed or anxious, you're normal and no less of a Christian. You may just need a little salt.

> Always laugh when you can, it is cheap medicine.
>
> — LORD BYRON

A CALL TO COURAGE

Show yourself kindness today. Maybe it's a trip to the doctor. Make the appointment. Do you need replenishment? Think back to things you used to enjoy before this chaos came into your life. Maybe watch a movie, read, have lunch with a friend (even if you cry), put together a puzzle, play a board game, take a bike ride, take a day trip, play the piano, bake a cake.

Take the advice of the Nike ad: Just Do It.

You'll be glad you did.

Chapter Eleven

ENLISTING HELP

> He heals the brokenhearted
> and binds up their wounds.
> *Psalm 147:3*

Four months following the Saturday that Sam moved out, I found myself two states away at a treatment center in Georgia, a residential center where he went to overcome pornography addiction. The center hosted Family Weekend so broken and skeptical families could rejoin their loved ones in hopes that life would be different.

While it was a family weekend, it wasn't kid friendly, so my hotel reservation was for one. Something I would have to get used to.

As I sat in the conference room before the first meeting, I glanced around to see regular people just like me. Hurting people. People whose lives had been wrecked by addiction, as a participant or a family member. My nerves were on edge, not knowing what to expect. What has been happening here for the last few months? Would things really be different this time?

Not only did I feel nervous, but sadness consumed me as I grieved all the things that could have been. Grieving the years wasted. Grieving the loss that was apparent simply by our living arrangements. We lived as strangers on a separate but together journey. How did we get here? How did we get from mission trips and anniversary getaways to a treatment center?

I knew how we had gotten there. A long and angry four-hour car ride had gotten us there three months earlier. Boy was I angry. So angry that the few words that came out of my mouth were drenched in hatefulness. His addiction had finally taken its toll on our family.

While I fought traffic and tears, Sam spent the four hours in the car writing notes to our children. He would have little to no contact with anyone outside of the treatment center for the first several weeks. Because communication was limited, he wrote notes for me to give to them each week. He wouldn't be home for Halloween. He also would miss Thanksgiving and Christmas. That would be the beginning of many firsts for us.

A treatment center would also be a first. Week-to-week counseling was no longer an option. He had done that already. You know the saying, "Desperate times call for desperate measures?" That's where we were. Desperate.

Desperate is how I felt when we pulled his bags out of the car and walked into the office. They were expecting him. He had done all the paperwork and made the arrangements. The time had come to make a bold and hopefully life-changing move.

When it was time to say goodbye, we hugged and cried not knowing what the future held. The goodbye was quick. No need to linger in the heartache. I took my place behind the steering wheel and started down the long, gravel driveway headed home. Alone. I gently waved goodbye and bit my quivering lip with no idea where this road would take us.

With tears rolling down my face questions rolled through my mind: Is this really happening? Is this my life? Will this finally be the thing that brings about change?

Through my tears, I managed Atlanta traffic which deserves a gold star any day. I finally made it to my hotel in South Carolina. I checked into my room eager for an emotional break and a good night's sleep.

I distinctly remember walking out of the hotel the next morning. I felt free. As I breathed in the fresh air, I said out loud, "It's a beautiful day to walk in freedom." That's how I felt. Free. That may sound harsh or cold but if you have lived with a person struggling with addiction, you can relate.

When I returned to the treatment center months later for Family Weekend, I joined other grief-stricken and broken people who came hopeful that this was the time chains of addiction were finally broken. Hesitant hope filled the room as we wondered if our lives could be normal again. These three days would start the process of restoring broken people and families.

Not only were family members there, but numerous counselors were on hand. Therapists who had spent months walking alongside men whose lives had been wrecked by addiction. Trained professionals who saw through the fake exterior to the broken people inside. Counselors who weren't afraid to confront the lies. Experts who were equipped and willing to help these men and their families walk through the mess poor choices and sin had taken them. These same people were helping families like ours put the pieces of our broken lives back together.

Another part of caring for ourselves is realizing we need help. There is no shame in needing people to help us sort out decisions and emotions. Sometimes it's too much for us to navigate ourselves. Our husbands aren't the only ones who need counselors. You and I need trained people to walk us through our pain so we can experience healing too. Psychologists, counselors/therapists, medical doctors, and pastors are all great places to look for guidance.

Finding a qualified counselor you connect with makes the healing process worthwhile. Not painless, but a journey worth taking. Counselors allow us to talk through issues, give us new perspectives, and offer coping skills from a neutral, trained source.

It is important to get qualified help. Wrong or unqualified guidance can leave us frustrated or feeling like it's our fault. Poor advice can loop us around cycles of defeat with no real progress forward. Examples of poor advice: just have sex more often, it's your fault, be more exciting in the bedroom, never say no, "boys will be boys." None of these things are true or helpful. Run for the hills if you receive this kind of advice.

For me, the most healing part of counseling was having my feelings validated. I experienced so much freedom in hearing a qualified person say that my experiences were valid and consistent with the wife of an addicted spouse. I didn't know I needed to hear that, but I did.

You may need to hear that too. You are not crazy and it's not your fault. There is a qualified someone out there who can listen to your pain, understand your experiences, and validate your feelings. I do hope you'll seek out a professional counselor to help you navigate this journey. I suggest a Certified Sex Addiction Therapist (CSAT).

I admit that counseling isn't convenient or cheap, but it is worth the juggling of schedules and every dime spent. I couldn't have made it through the first few months without my counselors reminding me of what is true. I learned to recognize distorted thinking and to let go of things I can't control. I gained confidence and learned to accept myself.

Everybody's counseling journey looks different. I am a do-er by nature. I like to get things done. As a do-er, I needed things to do in counseling to help me move forward.

For the first few months of counseling, Mona, my Christian counselor, sent me home with a worksheet in hand. I'd journal, reflect, pray, look up definitions then write some more. That's how I process. To this day, my favorite app is my dictionary app. I use it almost every day.

Looking up definitions doesn't sound therapeutic. To most, it probably isn't. But for me, having those definitions in hand gave me clarity to see myself, the good and the bad and everything in between. We can't change what we don't see or don't know.

Because I'm an (over) thinker, my CSAT, Stefanie, recommended an art project to use the creative side of my brain in the healing process. She asked me to create a separate art project for three different stages of my life: life before pornography addiction, life when pornography addiction was at its worst, and how I hoped my life would look after the dust settled. I still have those projects.

Whether you like art projects or worksheets or neither, please seek out the healing you deserve. As with medication, there can be a stigma associated with counseling but sometimes we need trained people to help us through a problem.

If we had a leak in our bathroom, we'd call a plumber. We may try fixing it with a few YouTube videos and pliers before we make the call. But when we've exhausted our options and efforts, we need qualified people to help fix our leak and our heart.

God is the Knower of all things. He doesn't need experts or skilled workers to accomplish His will yet when He wanted something built or made, He provided skilled workers for Moses:

> Then the Lord said to Moses, "See, I have chosen Bezalel son of Uri, the son of Hur, of the tribe of Judah, and I have filled him with the Spirit of God, with wisdom, with understanding, with knowledge and with all kinds of skills—to make artistic designs for work in gold, silver and bronze, to cut and set stones, to work in wood, and to engage in all kinds of crafts. Moreover, I have appointed Oholiab son of Ahisamak, of the tribe of Dan, to help him. Also I have given ability to all the skilled workers to make everything I have commanded you."
> *Exodus 31:1-6*

> "Tell all the skilled workers to whom I have given wisdom in such matters that they are to make garments for Aaron, for his consecration, so he may serve me as priest."
> *Exodus 28:3*

That's what counselors are—skilled workers who are equipped with wisdom and expertise. People who have been trained to help us navigate our pain. That's not to say God can't or won't use regular, everyday people in our healing. But sometimes we need a little skill to move us to the next level.

That's what happened at our Family Weekend. The counselors who had equipped our loved ones to manage their recovery shed light on how we too could move forward in our healing journey, one that would take longer than a four-hour car ride.

> The next best thing to being wise oneself is to live in a circle of those who are.
>
> — C.S. LEWIS

A CALL TO COURAGE

Evaluate your emotional state. Are you weepy? How is your sleep? Are you allowing yourself to grieve? Are you eating okay? Ask a friend for input and be honest with yourself. Also, take an intentional and courageous step to find a counselor, then schedule an appointment.

I suggest you consult a medical doctor before starting counseling to rule out anything medical that could be affecting the rest of life. Without a hypothyroidism diagnosis, Sam and I could have spent tons of time and hard-earned money on counseling in vain. No need to delay.

Chapter Twelve

THE FICKLENESS OF FEELINGS

> Every good and perfect gift is from above, coming down from the Father of the heavenly lights, who does not change like shifting shadows.
>
> *James 1:17*

During my separation, I shared plenty of meals with friends that led to a flood of tears. My heart was raw with emotion and the slightest thing could bring tears to my eyes. My tears flowed like a fountain drink.

At one such crying meal with a friend, she pointed out that I typically order the same thing to eat everywhere I go, some combination of soup, salad, or a sandwich. Unless, of course, it's Mexican, then it's a beef burrito with beans and no rice. Breakfast is no different. I eat the same thing most mornings too.

It seems I'm a creature of habit. I have chewed the same flavor of gum for years. I buy the same foods at the grocery store. I've been wearing the same eye cream since I was in my twenties. Now that I have a few decades under my belt, I might be due a little change. Change is hard even when it's good.

There is something to be said about sameness. It's safe and predictable. There's not a lot of guesswork or room for error when things stay the same. There is less danger in getting food you don't like or makeup that doesn't work. Sameness doesn't require risk.

Then there are things in life that change constantly. Things that are hard to pinpoint or predict. Technology tops the list. Just when you upgrade your phone, a newer model comes out. When you feel like you've mastered a computer program, an upgrade comes out. Seasons change, fashions change, and people change.

Out of all the things in this world that change, there is one thing I would put in the top ten list—feelings. They can be as unpredictable as rush hour and as up and down as a teeter-totter. Just ask any woman, or maybe her children.

What triggers feelings of happiness today may not crack a smile tomorrow. Things that made us cry yesterday may not trigger the slightest tear next week.

I imagine you and I are a lot alike. We may not chew the same flavor of gum but it's possible we have both been on the same roller coaster ride of emotions that comes with discovering our husband's pornography use. Even the steadiest of gals can be thrown for a loop when she discovers her husband's involvement with pornography. That means we're normal.

Feelings are a filter that affect how we experience our lives. I grew up with an awareness of three basic feelings—happy, sad, and mad. There might have been a couple more in the mix, but these were the big three. Minimal awareness and acknowledgement of feelings was our way of life. And feelings were kept inside so as not to complicate life.

Not showing feelings is hard for a girl who wears her heart on her sleeve. If I'm watching TV with my kids and something remotely touching comes on, they whip their heads around to see if my eyes look glassy with tears.

I managed my life and marriage on those three basic emotions. After counseling, and some worksheets, I managed to articulate more advanced feelings such as disregard and apathy. When Sam moved out, more feelings came rushing to the surface that didn't fall into those categories. My emotions were a jumbled mess. I truly had mixed feelings.

Perhaps you're feeling angry because of your husband's choices. You feel guilty because you don't want anything to do with him, but you're hopeful your marriage can be different now the truth is out. But when you think about it, the whole situation is depressing. That could happen while putting on mascara or picking up a package of his favorite snack at the grocery store.

Feelings can indicate what's happening on the inside but making decisions based on a feeling can cause mayhem on the outside. Feelings are good indicators but can't be relied on as good decision-makers. Feelings change with hormones, hunger, room temperature, surroundings, and circumstances.

It's one thing to order our food based on our feelings, but to order people around based on feelings can cause hurt, regret, and probably some tears. When someone hurts our feelings, oftentimes our reactions directed to unsuspecting people can leave a rift or have an unwanted domino effect.

Because feelings can skew the facts, it's in our best interest to try to separate feelings from facts, not perceived facts but actual facts. Considering how frequently feelings change, they cannot be trusted as truth tellers.

I'm not suggesting we dismiss our feelings and jump on the fact bandwagon. Dismissing our feelings will cause us to stagnate in healing. On the contrary, the more we can identify and educate ourselves on our feelings the clearer the picture becomes. Just reviewing a feelings wheel opened my eyes to more than your run-of-the-mill emotions.

Knowledge really is power. Knowing how we feel and why we feel it can be a powerful tool in healing. When we can pinpoint and articulate feelings, we have a place to start.

At our Family Weekend, each family member was offered the opportunity to express feelings about anything on our minds. At the beginning of each of the four meetings, we were offered the chance to stand, take the microphone (gulp), and express our hopes, reservations, and hurts. But we needed to phrase our emotions with a particular sentence structure, the same template our resident loved ones were trained to express their feelings at the start of their days. This was the template for our statements: I feel _____ about _____ because _____.

Each family member also was given extended time to sort out deeper feelings so we could articulate them in the same manner. We received a feelings wheel and sent on our way to dig deep. We were encouraged to say everything we needed to say because this may be the first time our loved one heard us.

I took my three basic emotions and my journal to McDonald's by the treatment center where I sat for two hours sorting out my feelings. I searched the feelings wheel looking for names of what was swirling around inside me. Did I feel abandoned, embarrassed, or frustrated? Or out of control, betrayed or infuriated? Or all the above?

I sat with my salad and water cup until I had identified every feeling and why I felt it. Identifying how I felt didn't make the heartache go away, but it gave me a means to express the heartache which gave me a clearer picture of my reality. The picture wasn't lovely, mind you, but at least it was clearer.

In regard to the fickleness of feelings, I want to encourage you with two things. First, Jesus never changes. While our emotions can change with the wind, Jesus is the same yesterday, today, and tomorrow. He is unchangeable and absolute.

Not only does God not change, but His feelings for us do not change. It's hard to believe God has feelings. He seems like this undefinable Being somewhere in the sky. But the Bible tells us that God rejoices (Zephaniah 3:17) and gets angry (2 Kings 21:6). He loves (John 3:16) and He laughs (Psalm 37:12-13). He feels compassion, pleasure, and grief (Psalm 103:13, 1 Kings 3:10, Psalm 78:40). And the shortest verse in the Bible shows Jesus weeping over the death of His friend whom He loved (John 11:35).

God loves us the same today when we got most things right as much as He did yesterday when we messed up miserably.

Second, because God doesn't change, we can. We don't have to stay stuck on the roller coaster of emotions. We don't have to cling to the same feelings we felt last month or last year. Jesus is the rock we stand on, the firm foundation that never changes. Because we have secure footing, we can step out to grow, change and learn.

His sameness is our springboard and our safety net. We can become more than we are because God is our constant. God can change our thoughts, moods, and desires. We can experience refreshing changes in our ideas, our bodies, and our emotions.

This 'adverse to change' girl doesn't want to go wild and crazy with too much change. If you and I meet for lunch, I will not be ordering the fish tacos or sushi, and I'll probably show up chewing cinnamon gum wearing Mary Kay eye cream.

> There is nothing permanent except change.
>
> — HERACLITUS

A CALL TO COURAGE

Spend time clarifying your feelings. No need to feel stressed about getting it right. This is simply a tool to help sort out your feelings.

Consult the emotions wheel included at the end of this chapter to help you think outside the usual emotions box. I've included some of my examples. Write as many as come to mind. This is a great skill to develop and revisit as often as necessary. Daily even.

I feel _________ about _________ because _________.

I feel helpless about your actions because there is nothing I can do or say to make you change, make better choices, or make you engage me.

I feel distant about our relationship because I had to choose distance to guard my heart, so I can be a healthy person.

I feel unimportant in our marriage because you have chosen pornography over me.

I feel discouraged about your actions because I see you continue to focus on yourself and your desires instead of cherishing our marriage and what we could be together.

I feel frustrated about your actions because of the countless cycles I have seen and experienced with you.

I feel skeptical about your recovery because I have heard many years of empty promises.

I feel disregarded and ignored about how you have treated me because you have continually and consistently excluded me from your life.

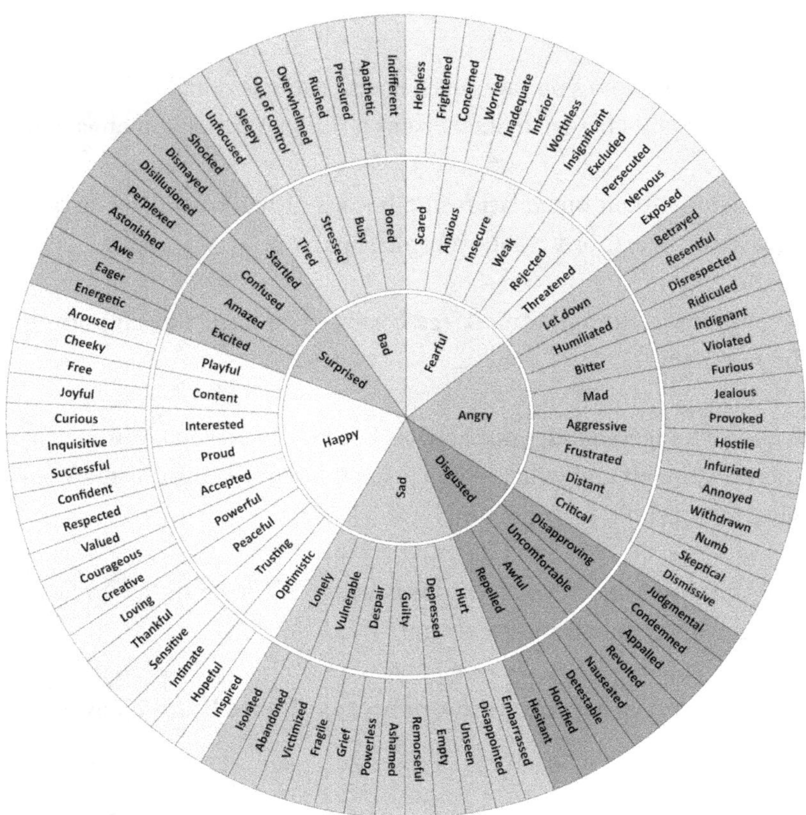

The above Emotions Wheel is provided courtesy of Geoffrey Roberts.

Chapter Thirteen

HIGHLY REGARDED

"The LORD your God is with you,
  the Mighty Warrior who saves.
He will take great delight in you;
  in his love he will no longer rebuke you,
  but will rejoice over you with singing."
Zephaniah 3:17

I like games—board games, card games, or any game, really. At our house we have stacks of games. During my separation Rene' often invited me over to play games. Nothing like a friendly game of Rummikub to distract you from reality for a bit. A little competition would momentarily take my mind off troubles and give my eyes a break from crying.

While I don't mind competition in games, I don't care for competition in marriage. I spent a lot of years competing in my marriage. Competing against countless women with perfect bodies in perfect lighting available any time of day at the click of a button. I, on the other hand, had birthed twins, wasn't much for tanning, and required seven hours of sleep.

I didn't realize I was in a competition, one I was losing. I knew something was off in my marriage, but I couldn't put my finger on it. I knew I didn't feel important, I just wasn't sure why. Every day, it seemed, I competed for time and affection.

Having to clamor your way to a person's heart can leave you feeling broken and disregarded. That's how I felt. Disregarded. I often felt like I didn't matter. I'm not saying we need the attention of our husbands 100 percent of the time, but we do deserve the devotion that comes along with our wedding vows.

Our fifteenth wedding anniversary tipped the disregard meter for me. Most years we went away for our anniversary, usually to the mountains. We'd shop, eat unhealthy food, relax, and sleep late—a nice break from bills, children, and routine. Some years were better than others, of course. But this year, the lack of attention finally got to me.

We took a risk and stayed at a new place I found online. We were looking for a peaceful place to land for a few days. The description fit the bill. A small cabin set off the road in quiet woods by a creek. Perfect. Almost. The cabin was indeed quaint and the surroundings beautiful, but there were no blinds and no heat. Well, to be fair, there was heat—a wood-burning stove. How did I miss that important detail in the online description?

Fortunately, Sam was a camper and a champ at building fires. He hauled in firewood and built a huge fire. Then it would get so hot we couldn't breathe. We'd have to open windows to let in some cool air, which was no problem since there were no blinds. But by morning, the fire would have died down and we'd wake up freezing.

Our relationship was a bit like the heat. Some days hot, some days cold. As of this trip, cold summed it up. I had never been married before, but I was kind of hoping for more on days than off days. At this point in our marriage, that was not the case. Pornography was luring him away.

For this anniversary trip I didn't pack any hobby things. No scrapbooking stuff or books or anything else I thought would distract me from investing in our relationship. I did, however, pack my expectations. I expected we would spend time together and focus on our marriage. We needed to. I assumed he thought the same thing since it was our anniversary.

I was wrong.

He brought his camera to practice photography. The scenic cabin setting offered countless opportunities for snapping stunning pictures. It became obvious that taking pictures was taking precedence over time with me. I was heartbroken.

While Sam was outside snapping pictures, I sat alone on the couch in the hot cabin. The coldness that had settled into our marriage settled into my heart. I grabbed my journal and scribbled: "Now I don't even care if I spend any time with him or not. I'm sad and hurt. We have 2 ½ days left on our trip plus the rest of our lives. Jesus, the truth is he hurt me, rejected me again, and that pushes me further away."

Have you been there? You feel rejected or disregarded, like you're second string when you know you should be the starter. The person you love and committed your life to doesn't love you back. It's painful when you don't feel worthy (enough) of someone else's time or attention.

While we may have lost the attention of our husbands, we have not and never will lose the attention of our God. I'm not saying we need to settle for less in our marriages; I am saying God always notices us. He truly sees us.

Psalm 34:15 tells us that "the eyes of the LORD are on the righteous. His ears are attentive to their cry." God is paying attention to you even if your husband is not. He sees you, not just your pain. He sees all of you. He notices you opening your Bible each day. He sees you trying to hold your tongue when you'd rather spout off hurtful words. He notices you faithfully taking your kids to school. He sees you trying hard to leave the last Oreo for somebody else.

There was a gal in the Bible trying hard to fly under the radar. You may remember her. She was the women with the issue of blood. Having a perpetual period for twelve years sounds like torture enough, but that also meant she was unclean. Nobody wanted anything to do with her. She was outcast and disregarded by most. Not to Jesus.

She had likely spent all her money, been to every doctor who would see her and was no better than she was a dozen years ago. Then Jesus came to town. Scores of people followed Him because they heard He can perform miracles. And that's what she needed, a miracle.

Jesus was her last-ditch effort. Her last hope. Her hope and determination pushed her toward Jesus. She knew if she could touch His robe, just the tip of it, she hoped she could finally be healed.

She risked more humiliation and pushed her unclean self through the crowd to get to Jesus, probably touching lots of clean people along the way. With all the faith she had in her bleeding body, her fingers touched the edge of his robe. Immediately she felt it. Healing. Instantly her bleeding stopped. Then the unthinkable happened.

Jesus noticed.

> Then Jesus asked, "Who was it who touched me?" When they all denied it, Peter said, "Master, the crowds are surrounding you and pressing against you!" But Jesus said, "Someone touched me, for I know that power has gone out from me." When the woman saw that she could not escape notice, she came trembling and fell down before him. In the presence of all the people, she explained why she had touched him and how she had been immediately healed. Then he said to her, "Daughter, your faith has made you well. Go in peace."
>
> *Luke 8:45-48 NET*

She could not escape notice. That is beautiful, isn't? She had been noticed by Jesus.

Jesus doesn't scold her for touching His robe or give her a good talking to in front of the crowd. She had already lived a decade being ostracized and outcast. Instead, He affectionately calls her, "Daughter." Jesus knew she not only needed to be cured, she needed to be cherished. At the sound of His voice, she went from a dirty, outcast woman to a treasured daughter.

Maybe your husband doesn't notice you or treats you like you don't matter. The days of you feeling cherished by him have long passed. Take heart, you are noticed. God hasn't forgotten you.

You are His treasured daughter, and you don't have to compete for His attention.

> A flower doesn't think of competing with the flower next to it. It just blooms.
>
> — ZEN SHIN

A CALL TO COURAGE

When we feel disregarded or unimportant, we can lose sight of the good parts of ourselves. Today recover the parts of you that have been buried under months or years of dismissal or disregard.

Make a list of ten things you like about yourself. Please don't skip this because it sounds cheesy. For example, are you a good listener? Do you have the gift of making people laugh? Can you string words together to encourage people?

Identify things you like about yourself. They might be buried in there somewhere. If you feel particularly down on yourself, ask a friend to point out things they like about you.

Now, relish in the fact that God made you and takes great delight in you!

Chapter Fourteen

SHIFTING OUR FOCUS

> Therefore, since we are surrounded by such a great cloud of witnesses, let us throw off everything that hinders and the sin that so easily entangles. And let us run with perseverance the race marked out for us, fixing our eyes on Jesus, the pioneer and perfecter of faith. For the joy set before him he endured the cross, scorning its shame, and sat down at the right hand of the throne of God.
>
> *Hebrews 12:1-2*

Over the last few years, I have learned a thing or two about myself. I have learned that I enjoy watching movies. I used to think they were a waste of two hours. I'm pretty picky about the movies I watch, but I have developed two personal policies: I don't drink out of water fountains, and I don't watch rated R movies.

I would have to be near dehydration to drink out of a water fountain, because at one of my son's soccer practices, I saw a boy washing his feet in the water fountain. I'm not a germaphobe but I prefer no feet with my water, please.

As for movies, the news offers enough R stuff for me.

One movie I have loved for years is *The Wizard of Oz*. Poor Dorothy is stuck in Oz with a bunch of weirdos desperately trying to get home. She grew to love her strange companions as they set out on a quest to find the Wizard of Oz so he could send her back to normal life in Kansas.

The yellow brick road takes her and her odd companions to the Wizard of Oz where Toto, the brave terrier hero, pulls back the curtain on the wizard and exposes him for what he really is—a regular man with a giant microphone. When this regular man posing as a wizard sees he has been found out, he frantically pulls the curtain around him and yells, "Pay no attention to that man behind the curtain."

But it was too late. He had been exposed for what he really was: a humbug, if I may use Scarecrow's description. Dorothy and her friends were disappointed to see he was not a wizard at all. He was a fraud. A deceiver.

The truth is we, too, have a deceiver. Someone behind the person, behind the hurtful words and bad choices. Someone behind the curtain. His name is Satan.

He is not a bumbling lion like the sweet lion in Oz. He's a different lion entirely. He is the father of lies roaming the earth like a roaring lion looking for someone to devour. Make no mistake, we have an enemy who is seeking to steal our hope and destroy our marriage. A roaring lion who is champing at the bits to devour the last shred of faith we have in restoring our marriage.

And he is desperately hoping we won't notice him. If he can keep us distracted into thinking people in our lives are the enemy, he keeps winning. I don't know about you, but I'm tired of losing. You and I have lost so much already.

It's easier for us to look at the outside of our husbands, or anybody that pushes our buttons, and think they're the enemy. It sure feels true. When we are deeply wounded it is easy to see others who hurt us or don't share our opinion as the enemy. Or we can get so ticked off and forget we have an enemy.

I have been there more times than I can count. It's easier to be mad at a person with skin on. But what if we somehow pried our eyes away from our husband's wrongdoings to see we have an enemy—a bona fide, legit enemy.

I'm not offering a free pass to our husbands for their involvement with pornography or dismissing their ability to choose. I'm suggesting there may be a better way for us to get through our overwhelming days. A healthier way to use the last shred of our energy than focusing on another person.

Where we choose to focus is essential to our healing. Athletes understand the importance of focus. Do you watch the Olympics? When it's on TV we usually watch it because it is mostly decent. The last time the winter Olympics were on, my daughter was inspired by the ice skaters and decided she wanted to go ice skating. So, one Sunday afternoon I begrudgingly gave up my Sunday afternoon nap and hauled off to the ice-skating rink. I shelled out $20, we laced up our skates, and cautiously took to the ice.

Ice skating can't be that hard, right? Instead of gracefully sashaying around the ice like Michelle Kwan, I slowly stomped around the rink flailing my arms. I had two goals: not to fall and not to hit people with my arms. Lofty goals.

A silver lining clearly exists in slow, unskilled ice skating. Eavesdropping. I know. Don't judge. As I shuffled by a man teaching his son to skate, I overheard him offer skating advice to the little guy. "Stop looking at your feet and start looking where you're going." It seemed simplistic, but I had nothing better going for my skating career, so I tried it.

I shifted my focus from my feet to the rink before me. Wouldn't you know it, it worked. When I changed where I put my gaze, skating was not only easier but much more enjoyable. My stomping turned into spurts of gliding.

Changing my gaze didn't change my reality. I was still on thin blades, on slippery ice with people whizzing by me, but my shift in focus changed how I experienced my reality.

But I had to choose to shift my focus.

We can intentionally shift our gaze choosing not to focus on our husband and his failings or the enemy and his lies. There is a better way to get through our days, to get through the pain and heartache. Let's turn our eyes to a different Lion altogether.

Revelation 5 calls Jesus the Lion of the tribe of Judah. What if we shifted our attention to Jesus? The One who put on human flesh and willingly came to a broken world knowing He would be rejected, tortured, and nailed to a cross. The One who loves people who are far from God so they can come near. The One who gives hope to those of us who have circumstances in our lives that seem hopeless. Jesus.

Shifting our focus to Jesus doesn't mean we have to act happy, or we stop crying, or the pain magically goes away. But choosing to focus on the Problem Solver instead of the problem can bring a glimpse of hope to our long days and broken hearts.

The Israelites had some long days too. Because of their disobedience, their forty-day trip to the Promised Land turned into a forty-year trip filled with more disobedience and a whole lot of camping.

On their wilderness journey God provided a cloud to guide them by day and a fire to give them light and guide them by night. The cloud and the fire rested over the Tent of Meeting, a portable sanctuary where God's presence dwelled.

When the cloud or fire moved, that was their signal to break camp and move with God. When the cloud or fire stopped, the Israelites stopped and set up camp for as long as the cloud or fire remained.

A seasoned camper will tell you that there are certain guidelines you need to know when camping. For example, check the weather. Take a first aid kit. Don't leave your fire unattended or leave trash out unless you're interested in furry visitors.

God gave the Israelites specific instructions on setting up their camp.

> The LORD spoke to Moses and Aaron, saying, "The people of Israel shall camp each by his own standard, with the banners of their fathers' houses. They shall camp facing the tent of meeting on every side."
> *Numbers 2:1-2*

God instructed Moses to arrange the Israelites in a specific order around the Tent of Meeting so that He was the focal point. The Tent of Meeting was always the center with the twelve tribes of Israel positioned around it. Having Him in the center was their not-so-subtle reminder of Who was leading the way.

Some commentaries say this arrangement placed God's people in the shape of a T, like a cross, a foreshadowing to Jesus and His death on the cross. The Tent of Meeting served as their focal point just as Jesus is our focus as twenty-first century believers.

Like a campfire placed strategically in the center, Jesus is the light in our darkness. He is the anchor we can build our lives around. And He is the One leading our way.

He may not change our circumstances. To be clear, He is certainly able. Perhaps He wants to change us during our circumstances.

You and I didn't choose our situation, but we are free to choose where we put our focus. Shifting our gaze to Jesus may not change our reality. We still have a battle to fight, hard stuff to sort out, and decisions to make, but it will change us in our reality.

Having an enemy is part of our reality. Let's pull back the curtain and expose him. He is a defeated foe. His power is limited. He is a loser and not worth our attention.

It is during our darkest moments that we must focus to see the light.

— ARISTOTLE ONASSIS

A CALL TO COURAGE

Has the enemy distracted you? It's time to shift our focus. Crank up some worship music and focus on the Problem Solver. Don't read the Bible or ask God for stuff. Just listen to the words of the songs and worship from your mouth and your heart.

Chapter Fifteen

GOD OF WONDERS

And God is able to bless you abundantly, so that in all things at all times, having all that you need, you will abound in every good work.
2 Corinthians 9:8

The craziest thing happened one day while Sam was away at the treatment center. My kids and I were coming home from a gymnastics class. For my daughter, not me, although I can still do a mean cartwheel. Just one. As we turned on our road, I noticed a woman sitting in a car parked in front of our house. Not knowing who it was, I hesitated to pull into the driveway.

Having watched most episodes of *Wonder Woman* in my younger years, I figured I could probably take her, so I pulled into the driveway. When I got out of the car the driver also exited her car. She looked vaguely familiar. I sent my children inside and walked to meet her. She introduced herself, and I realized she was one of Sam's coworkers and we exchanged a few sentences.

She went on to express how hard it must be for Sam to be away, for us not to know if he had enough sick time to cover his absence from work and me not have a job. Well, a paying job. Motherhood is quite the job, but it doesn't pad the bank account. Then she offered me an envelope. I thanked her profusely, and we parted ways.

I went inside, opened the envelope, and cried. She had just given us $1,000 cash. Not from their employer, from her personally. That's a wonder woman if I've ever seen one.

This is one of countless stories of God's overt provision for us on our journey. I have been in awe over the creative ways God has met our needs. It goes way beyond finances. But I cannot honestly share about my experience without including a chapter on how God financially provided for us. I know. It sounds boring. Blah, blah, blah.

Nobody really wants to talk about the state of the checkbook much less share it with the world. Money is one touchy subject, especially if we don't have much money to touch. But we all need money. It's possible you're independently wealthy or won the lottery and aren't in need of cash. If that's you, I'm grateful for generous people like you who help regular people like me. Thank you. For the rest of us, moolah might be in a little higher demand.

When we hear stories of how God provides, it is easy to tune it out and think God only does that for other people. I'm here to tell you that is a big, fat lie. God can, and does, provide for people every single day. He may not drop bundles of cash from the sky, but the truth is there are nice, generous people all over this planet, not just in the town I live in.

I imagine you're in the same boat we were in. The low on cash, high in need boat. We spent our savings on treatment, counseling, and things necessary for healing. Sometimes crying over Mexican food with a friend is oddly necessary.

I struggled with using our savings because, doggone it, it takes so long to save money. If we exhausted our savings, an emergency might pop up. The car could break down or somebody might need surgery. Both were likely at our house.

Without savings we'd be in bad shape. The truth is we were already in bad shape. The transmission hadn't fallen out of one of our cars, but the life had been drained out of our marriage. That was an emergency far greater than a car repair. An emergency worth investing in.

It's easy to say with our mouths how important our marriage and family are but sometimes God asks us to say it with our checkbook.

We hesitantly emptied most of our savings in search of healing for our family. I can't say we did it with great joy or because we are super godly. We did it because we were desperate, and it seemed like the only way forward. I can say without hesitation that I would do it all over again. Every penny spent was worth it. I can also say without hesitation that I would be happy to not have to do it all over again.

When Sam and I went through premarital counseling, we did an assessment that measured what our strengths and weaknesses might be in our marriage. Our assessment indicated that finances could be a struggle for us. The assessment was spot on.

Our family backgrounds were vastly different when it came to handling finances. He came from a family of budget balancers. My family's idea of balancing a checkbook is putting it on your finger and if it doesn't fall off, then it's balanced.

But for the decision on how to heal our family we were on the same ledger page. We knew it would cost us—both time and money. And money that doesn't grow on trees, but it does sometimes show up in your mailbox.

Do you have a mailbox checker at your house? Someone who consistently checks the mail. I love checking the mail. It's like opening a present every day. Thanks to Amazon prime we can have presents delivered seven days a week.

The mailbox checker at our house is my daughter. I prefer checking the mail but since I'm the adult I let her check it. Not long after Sam moved out, Grace returned from the mailbox one day with an anonymous looking card addressed to me. There was no return address, and my name and address were typed instead of handwritten.

I tore open the envelope. We aren't classy or patient enough at our house to use a letter opener. Inside I found an unsigned card and a gift card to Walmart. I turned over the card and envelope looking for a clue as to who it was from. Nothing. Some anonymous person thought enough about us to take a trip to the store, buy a gift card, print out an address label, and mail it to us. Who does that?

More amazingly, this went on for five years! I still don't know who it is. It didn't happen every day or every month, but three or four times a year we opened the mailbox to find a gift card from this mysterious person. It has been the coolest thing for my kids and me to see God meet our needs in such a creative way. It is tangible proof that God hasn't forgotten us. He is taking fine care of us.

And He can do the same for you. Don't let anyone tell you otherwise. An anonymous person may not send you mail, or someone may not show up in your driveway with an envelope of cash. Or maybe they will. How ever God chooses to meet your needs will be a reminder that His heart toward you is good. That He is good, and greater than any heartache or need we have.

The servants at the wedding in Cana had a need of their own. In the second chapter of John, we read how the wedding hosts ran out of wine for their guests. To alleviate embarrassment of the host, Mary, the mother of Jesus, did what most moms do. She offered her son to help.

We've all volunteered our kids to do something. That's what Mary did. She told the servants to do whatever Jesus said. Since Jesus is a fan of the Ten Commandments, He was careful to honor His mom. Then Jesus turned water into wine.

Not just any old wine. He gave them exceptional wine that did more than meet the requirement for their guests. He went above and beyond because that's who He is. And that is who He can be for you too.

What do you need? A job or money to pay the mortgage, buy gas, or pay for counseling. Shoes for a growing kid. Maybe you need less tangible things like energy to get out of bed, a good night's sleep, or focus at work.

That tank of gas or counseling session may seem like a far reach for you, but not to the God who owns it all. What seems impossible to us doesn't make a dent in God's bank account. Oprah's Favorite Things episodes might get more press, but God has more than cars, vacations, and KFC to give away.

Whatever your need, be prepared for His creativity. He may meet your needs in ways you never considered. Then you and I can meet for ice cream and swap stories of God's generosity.

It wasn't a walk down Easy Street for us as I'm sure it isn't for you either. Sometimes it has been more like walking a tightrope. Yes, my car has broken down, we have had tight months and have gone without. But God has wowed us with His generous heart through generous people.

As much as I'd like to be Wonder Woman, it's God who is the wonder. The One who wows us with His presence, His provision, and His power. And you know what? I think He enjoys every minute of it.

> All I have needed Thy hand hath provided. Great is Thy faithfulness, Lord unto me.
>
> — THOMAS CHISHOLM

A CALL TO COURAGE

It's your turn. Make a list of your needs. It can be as long as it needs to be. Don't hold back. With list in hand, ask God to open the windows of heaven and pour out His blessings of provision on you.

I cannot guarantee He will answer 'yes' to all your requests, but I can guarantee He will hear you.

And He just might do more than you can imagine.

Chapter Sixteen

SELFIE

Let us examine our ways and test them,
and let us return to the LORD.
Lamentations 3:40

Prior to my Dr. Jekyll, Mr. Hyde experience, Sam and I had already been to marriage counseling. We scraped together the money, found a sitter, and off we went looking for answers. During our sessions I learned a lot about myself. I'd like to say I discovered how loving and kind I am and how words flow from my tongue with grace and ooze with gentleness. I could tell you that but then I'd be a liar too.

And that is not the picture I saw when I looked in the mirror. It's the reflection I'd like to see. I do see that person sometimes. But other times the person looking back at me isn't who I want to be.

I want the person in my mirror to be warm, thoughtful, and equipped with the upmost patience. Sometimes my reflection shows a different person. A stranger even. A person whose critical tongue and harsh words can pierce an already wounded heart. I am definitely not the fairest one of all.

Dealing with our own stuff, our own faults and tendencies can cause us to buck up on the inside and demand our rights. Or maybe it's just me. Pride can rear its head and say, "I'm not the one looking at pornography." And you're absolutely right.

When our husband takes his past and dumps it into our present, it hurts. Terribly. The last thing we want to do is consider our issues. So, if you're not there yet, that is a-okay. We're all at different parts of our journey. Some are in crisis mode while others have been on the journey a little longer. If you're not there, skip this chapter and circle back later when you don't need twenty-four-hour access to a tissue box.

When shock and anger eventually lessen, it becomes necessary to take a look at ourselves. To peek in the mirror at our issues and ask God to tenderly show us areas in our hearts that may need some attention. I'm not suggesting we need one of those mirrors that magnifies ten times the actual size. Not that kind. Let's start with a little peek in the mirror of God's Word.

James 1:25 says, "But whoever looks intently into the perfect law that gives freedom and continues in it—not forgetting what they have heard but doing it—they will be blessed in what they do."

Like you I could use some freedom and blessing in my life. But looking into God's Word and seeing my imperfections can be difficult. It's more flattering to measure ourselves against others who appear less than perfect.

The truth is: God is for us. His Word is meant to lift us up, not beat us down. When we look in The Word and see parts of ourselves that need work, we are given the opportunity to adjust our attitudes, thoughts, and actions. It is through that adjustment that we experience freedom. Freedom from the things that hinder our relationship with Him and others. Yes, God is for us, but He is not for us staying the same. He wants much more for us.

I'll be the first to admit, it would be more pleasant to skip the self-evaluation and live in ignorant bliss about our issues. To keep ourselves blind to our blind spots. But no healing can be complete without an honest look at ourselves. No change can happen until we know what needs changing.

Author and founder of QBQ, Inc., John G. Miller says it well:

"God, grant me the serenity to accept the people I cannot change, the courage to change the one I can, and the wisdom to know it's me."

After Sam moved out, his issues were exposed for others to see. While I grieved, ugly cried, and went to counseling, my issues surfaced too. Please hear me. My issues did not cause him to make his choices. They were his choices. But I do have to take responsibility for me.

When my anger started to let up a little, and it took a while, and I was able to take my eyes off my husband, I learned some hard realities about myself. You know the saying, "Confession is good for the soul but bad for the reputation?" Well, I'm about to tank my reputation.

There are three areas of my life that God gently pried open my eyes to see. I hope they don't apply to you but if they do maybe we can have coffee. Or maybe just water since I'm not a coffee drinker. But not from a water fountain.

First, I'm not always right. *Drats!* I don't know about you, but I like being right. I'd like to gloss over that and move on to less prideful things. I really would. I am coming to terms with my ridiculous need to be right. The problem with always being right is that I'm wrong sometimes. Wrong about people's motives, wrong about how I remember things, and wrong about what time Walmart opens. Sometimes I'm just wrong. Period. That covers it.

As if being wrong isn't troubling enough to work through, there is blind spot number two: I am not perfect. That may not come as a shock to you, but it was an eye-opener to me. Not that I really thought I was perfect in every sense of the word like Jesus, but I tried so hard to do everything perfectly. To do everything right.

As much as I try to do everything right, I mess up. One time I proofed notecards for work and ordered the cards. The 500 notecards arrived with an eleven-digit telephone number. Yep, an eleven-digit phone number. Not ten digits. That was a big mess up.

When we open up about our struggles it takes away any doubt as to our level of imperfection. We work hard to look like we have it together. We want to be like Mary Poppins, "practically perfect in every way." But we're not. Perfectionism is an elusive, unattainable goal. A goal we often want for ourselves and expect from other people.

And the final reputation crusher brings me back to the part about having a sharp tongue and using critical words. During a heart-to-heart conversation with one of my kids, they said, "I feel like you're always looking at our flaws and our faults." Those painful words were not said hatefully but with respect from a sincere heart. Honestly, I needed to hear it. I needed to be reminded that my words and tone of voice can tear down or lift up other people. I really want to be a lifter-upper.

Sometimes I'm a fixer-upper. Fixing myself and others up. Always looking for better, more efficient ways to be better and do better. But, you know, not everybody enjoys a little helpful criticism, especially if you're a teenager. Sometimes I think I'm pushing my kids or others to be better when I'm actually pushing them away.

Instead of loving people for who they are, I think, "Let me help you be a better version of you, even if you don't think you need help or want to change." What that really says is, "You're not good enough." I presume to know what would be better. Better usually means more like me.

When I constantly evaluate and point out things that could be better or different in myself or others, I miss the opportunity to love. God tells us to love your neighbor as yourself, not fix your neighbor to be like yourself.

For all our faults, failures, and mistakes God still loves us. He loves us enough to keep us from camping out there too long. If we see characteristics in our mirror that make us look human, that's because we are. Humans with sins and flaws that Jesus died for. If we were perfect, we wouldn't need a Savior to save us from ourselves and help us choose the kind of human we want to be.

We are one choice away from the person we want to be. Just one. When we choose self-control or patience or kindness once, that means we can do it again. And again, and again. The more we choose those things the more we look like Jesus. You and I will never be the fairest one of all because Jesus already is. Sorry, Snow White.

But we can make choices in a way the causes what we see in our mirror to be a reflection of Jesus.

What's in your mirror?

> Have courage and be kind.
>
> — CINDERELLA'S MOTHER

A CALL TO COURAGE

Below is a list of fifteen types of distorted thinking, stinkin' thinkin' if you will. These are similar to the worksheet I worked through with my counselor.*

Mark the ones you recognize in your own thinking. Be honest. Honesty is the only way we can move forward. If you have marked several, don't be discouraged. You are not flying solo.

Let's own our stinkin' thinkin', but let's not stay there. Acknowledge it and ask God to help you overcome it. Day by day. One thought at a time.

_____ 1. Filtering
We take the negative details and magnify them while filtering out all positive aspects of a situation.

For instance, a person may pick out a single, unpleasant detail and dwell on it exclusively so their vision of reality becomes distorted.

_____ 2. Polarized Thinking (or "Black and White" Thinking)
Here, things are either "black-or-white." We have to be perfect or we're a failure. There is no middle ground. You place people or situations in "either/or" categories, with no shades of gray. If your performance falls short of perfect, you see yourself as a total failure.

---

* Sandra Silva, "How to Identify Cognitive Distortions: Examples and Meaning," *Psych-Central*, Updated Nov. 22, 2024, https://psychcentral.com/lib/cognitive-distortions-negative-thinking#definition, (accessed 01/15/25).

______ 3. Overgeneralization
In this cognitive distortion, we come to a general conclusion based on a single incident or a single piece of evidence. If something bad happens only once, we expect it to happen over and over again. A person may see a single, unpleasant event as part of a never-ending pattern of defeat.

______ 4. Jumping to Conclusions
Without individuals saying so, we know what they are feeling and why they act the way they do. We are able to determine how people feel toward us.

For example, a person may conclude that someone is reacting negatively toward them but doesn't bother to find out if they are correct.

Another example is a person may anticipate that things will turn out badly and will feel convinced their prediction is already an established fact.

______ 5. Catastrophizing
We expect disaster to strike, no matter what. We hear about a problem and use what if questions: "What if tragedy strikes?" or "What if it happens to me?"

For example, a person might exaggerate the importance of insignificant events (such as their mistake, or someone else's achievement). Or they may inappropriately shrink the magnitude of significant events until they appear tiny (a person's desirable qualities or someone else's imperfections).

______ 6. Personalization
Personalization is a distortion in which a person believes that everything others do or say is some kind of direct, personal reaction to the person. We also compare ourselves to others trying to determine who is smarter, better looking, etc. A person engaging in personalization may also see themselves as the cause of some unhealthy external event that they were not responsible for.

For example, "We were late to the dinner party and caused the host to overcook the meal. If I had only pushed my husband to leave on time, this wouldn't have happened."

______ 7. Control Fallacies
If we feel 'externally controlled,' we see ourselves as a helpless victim of fate.

For example, "I can't help it if the quality of the work is poor, my boss demanded I work overtime on it."

The fallacy of 'internal control' has us assuming responsibility for the pain and happiness of everyone around us. For example, "Why aren't you happy? Is it because of something I did?"

______ 8. Fallacy of Fairness
We feel resentful because we think we know what is fair, but other people won't agree with us. As our parents tell us when we're growing up and something doesn't go our way, "Life isn't always fair." People who go through life applying a measuring ruler against every situation judging its 'fairness' will often feel bad and negative because of it. Because life isn't 'fair'—things will not always work out in your favor, even when you think they should.

______ 9. Blaming
We hold other people responsible for our pain or take the other track and blame ourselves for every problem.

For example, "Stop making me feel bad about myself!" Nobody can 'make' us feel any particular way. Only we have control over our emotions and emotional reactions.

______ 10. Shoulds

We have a list of ironclad rules about how others and we should behave. People who break the rules make us angry, and we feel guilty when we violate these rules. A person may often believe they are trying to motivate themselves with 'shoulds' and 'shouldn'ts,' as if they have to be punished before they can do anything.

For example, "I really should exercise. I shouldn't be so lazy." 'Musts' and 'oughts' are also offenders. The emotional consequence is guilt. When a person directs 'should' statements toward others, they often feel anger, frustration, and resentment.

______ 11. Emotional Reasoning

We believe that what we feel must be true automatically. If we feel stupid and boring, we must be stupid and boring. You assume that your unhealthy emotions reflect the way things really are.

For example, "I feel it; therefore, it must be true."

______ 12. Fallacy of Change

We expect that other people will change to suit us if we just pressure or cajole them enough. We need to change people because our hopes for happiness seem to depend entirely on them.

______ 13. Global Labeling

We generalize one or two qualities into a negative global judgment. These are extreme forms of generalizing and are also referred to as 'labeling' and 'mislabeling.' Instead of describing an error in context of a specific situation, a person will attach an unhealthy label to themselves.

For example, they may say, "I'm a loser" in a situation where they failed at a specific task. When someone else's behavior rubs a person the wrong way, they may attach an unhealthy label to him, such as "He's a real jerk."

Mislabeling involves describing an event with language that is highly colored and emotionally loaded. For example, instead of saying someone drops her children off at daycare every day, a person who is mislabeling might say that "she abandons her children to strangers."

______ 14. Always Being Right
We are continually on trial to prove that our opinions and actions are correct. Being wrong is unthinkable, and we will go to any length to demonstrate our rightness.

For example, "I don't care how badly arguing with me makes you feel, I'm going to win this argument no matter what because I'm right." Being right often is more important than the feelings of others.

______ 15. Heaven's Reward Fallacy
We expect our sacrifice and self-denial to pay off, as if someone is keeping score. We feel bitter when the reward doesn't come.

Chapter Seventeen

MORE THAN SQUEAKING BY

> "When you pass through the waters,
>   I will be with you;
> and when you pass through the rivers,
>   they will not sweep over you.
> When you walk through the fire,
>   you will not be burned;
>   the flames will not set you ablaze."
> *Isaiah 43:2*

When Sam and I first got married I convinced myself that I liked camping, that pitching a tent at a primitive site at the campground close to our house was my idea of a fun weekend. What's not to like about the beauty of the outdoors, a babbling brook, and a campfire complete with s'mores? All that sounded peaceful.

One weekend we tested our camping limits and went with my friend Becky, her husband, and our dogs. We hiked what seemed like 700 miles to our campsite, set up our tents, and chatted around the campfire. Then bedtime came. Before we went to bed, we had to hoist our food up in a tree, so the bears didn't eat it. No one told me there would be bears. And they climb trees. And if bears can get in coolers, it seems one swipe of their paws can take down the thin nylon fortress called a tent.

During another camping trip following our suspended food adventure, I laid in our tent one evening listening to creepy creatures, sweating profusely, and wishing I had packed an air mattress instead of the thin roll-up mat from Walmart. That night I had an epiphany—just as Sam-I-Am does not like green eggs and ham, Jody Allen does not like camping.

Some of us in this great big world prefer a controlled climate, sleeping without bugs, and not having to walk in the dark while being stalked by bears to get to the bathroom. I might be more suited for glamping. Who am I kidding? Let's go straight to the Marriott.

As if bugs, humidity, and the long trek to the bathroom aren't enough reasons to stay in the comfort of your air-conditioned home, there is the issue of the campfire. While I love the heat from a fire on a cold day and the peaceful crackle of wood, I don't love the smell of campfires. After an evening around a campfire or making s'mores in the backyard my hair and clothes smell like smoke. A scent that lingers for days unless I hop in the shower and throw my clothes in the washer right away.

Pro tip for non-campers: Try Woodwick candles. Since the wicks are made from wood they crackle like a campfire. You can burn them in the comfort of your bug-free home like a regular candle. Which means you can enjoy the crackling of a campfire with the smell of Warm Woods without actually being in the woods.

Just as the smell of smoke tends to linger after spending time around a campfire, I want to navigate through this heartbreak without lingering bitterness or resentment. Or unforgiveness permeating my relationships or shame holding me back from the life God has for me. I don't want that for you either.

We've all seen it before. A person or a family goes through a terrible time. Maybe a person leaves this world far too early or there has been some sort of trauma or even divorce. That tragedy leaves broken people in its wake. People who are devastated, confused, or angry. And rightfully so! Sometimes that trauma or heartbreak can hold them captive for the rest of their lives causing a domino effect in their relationships, finances, or career.

When we were abruptly thrust into this journey, I made up my mind from the beginning that I didn't want to end up bitter, crippled by a lifetime of poor decisions, or crying every day. Okay, crying every day might be okay since there are some heartwarming commercials. I wanted to get through to the other side and be a whole person. Not just a whole person but a person who had gone through something hard, learned some lessons, and turned out just fine.

I didn't want to just survive. I didn't want my kids to just survive either. I wanted us to thrive. To take the hand dealt to us and allow God to use it to make us stronger and better and healthier. I don't want my future to be solely defined by my past.

As we look back on the life of King Nebuchadnezzar, we see that he built a gold statue and required all the people in his kingdom to bow to his god. There were three guys who would have no part in it, Shadrach, Meshach, and Abednego. Because they refused to bow to the king's god, they were punished by being cast into the fiery furnace to be burned alive.

> Nebuchadnezzar then approached the opening of the blazing furnace and shouted, "Shadrach, Meshach and Abednego, servants of the Most High God, come out! Come here!"
>
> So Shadrach, Meshach and Abednego came out of the fire, and the satraps, prefects, governors and royal advisers crowded around them. They saw that the fire had not harmed their bodies, nor was a hair of their heads singed; their robes were not scorched, and there was no smell of fire on them.
>
> *Daniel 3:26-27*

The fire didn't touch them. Their hair and clothes were untouched by a fire that had killed the men who had thrown them in. They weren't just untouched by the fire, they didn't even smell like smoke! Not even a hint. They literally had been through the fire and came out on the other side without the slightest stench of smoke. Their time in the fire left them with a story without the stench.

Let that be us. Let's not bend our knee to permanent despair, fear, anger, or anything that may cause the world around us to smell the stench of the enemy on us. Let's choose to bend our knee to the only One who can set us free from the things that hold us back. That can be us. We can be the one who gets through to the other side better, stronger, and healthier, even if we don't like how it turns out.

Working with a Certified Sex Addiction Therapist is one way I grew stronger and healthier. I highly recommend a CSAT for spouses of pornography addicts. In one of our sessions, she asked me to write a letter to sex addiction. I scoffed. It sounded a little kooky at first. It still does. But writing that letter reminded me that my life doesn't have to be defined by this heartbreak.

This is what I wrote:

Dear Sex Addiction,

You have profoundly and negatively affected my life. You have used your oppressive tentacles to maneuver yourself into the marrow of my marriage, tainting the very gift given by God to create oneness. You have authored lies, sucked away trust, and placed an enormous wedge in my relationship with Sam. It is because of you that we have endured the pain of separation and the unknowns of the future.

At your hands I have experienced betrayal beyond words, rejection, immense disregard along with mountains of irritation and anger. You have stolen years that can never be replaced. You have broken trust that will take years to rebuild.

And it isn't just my life and family you have affected. You have preyed on vulnerable and broken people to draw them into your deadly clutches. You have used your most valuable tool, pornography, to deceive even the strongest man into thinking he has it all under control and that there is no harm in what he is doing. You have used these vulnerable and captive people to fuel a worldwide epidemic of people enslaved to sex, damaging lives, destroying families, and distorting the gift given to create intimacy. Your insidious and deceptive nature has created heinous markets where prostitution, child pornography, and sex-trafficking are acceptable forms of capitalism. Not only do you deceive consumers, but you shamelessly exploit innocent people for your gain. I am repulsed by you!

Lest you think the only things you have contributed to my life are negative, that is not so! What I have gained while dealing with you is more strength than I ever thought possible. My faith has blossomed, and I have learned to dig in my heels and press on with determination. While it may appear from the outside that you have won, I assure you, with great confidence, that indeed you have not won. You may continue your rampage of consuming and destroying the lives of many people, but I emphatically refuse to allow that to be true of my life. The things you have taken away are slowly being replaced by greater and better things. Things that have only been possible by my encounter with you. So, it is with one word I leave you, "Checkmate!"

I'm not much of a chess player, but I do know checkmate is the end of the line. Game over. The time where the victory dance happens. You and I may not be to the victory dance part yet, but it's coming. If we refuse to allow the enemy to taint our lives with his lies, we have a victory dance coming our way.

While Shadrach, Meshach, and Abednego were in the fire something peculiar happened to them that I hope happens to us. They entered the fiery furnace bound but walked out of the fire free, unbound by the chains meant to ensure their death.

Oh, that you and I would emerge from this fire free, unbound by things that hold us back, create havoc in our lives, or cause us to doubt. Just as there was a fourth Person in the fire with them, we have Someone in the fire with us. Jesus. He is the One who can free us from our bondage and rid us of the stench the enemy wants to leave in our lives.

Let's ask God to give us the courage to dig in our heels and press on with determination. We are not wandering around the fire alone.

We are not defeated. Yes, we'll have days when we struggle with self-worth, anger, or other human things, but we don't have to allow our future to be defined by our past.

And while those are normal human struggles we need to deal with, we don't have to camp there.

> A woman is like a tea bag – you can't tell how strong she is until you put her in hot water.
>
> — ELEANOR ROOSEVELT

A CALL TO COURAGE

If you feel a little daring today, how about writing a letter to sex addiction or pornography? Remind yourself that stench-free living is possible.

Chapter Eighteen

TRADING THIS FOR THAT

> For you know the grace of our Lord Jesus Christ, that though he was rich, yet for your sake he became poor, so that you through his poverty might become rich.
> *2 Corinthians 8:9*

Every Sunday night for two years after Sam moved out, you could find my kids and me in the same place, at home sitting on the couch watching TV. Life had dealt us some hard blows and we needed a break from the hard stuff. Laughter seemed like good medicine, so *America's Funniest Home Videos* became a staple in our weekly routine.

Bennett and Grace scurried around to get ready for bed so they could jump in their beds when the credits rolled. We'd pack lunches and brush teeth during commercials then laugh until our cheeks hurt.

Sunday nights were a bright spot in our week, a time to leave our sorrows in the other room and laugh. We traded our sorrows in for a little laughter. Trading our tears for a few giggles didn't change our circumstances, but those belly laughs helped us press pause on the hard stuff to make space for something happier, even if it was only temporary.

Trading happens all around us from Wall Street to our street. You and I make trades all the time. We swap cash for clothes and skills for a paycheck. The finance world is chock-full of traders. Professional organizers trade clutter for cleanliness. And we trade our time for sleep, hobbies, and work. On a good day, we may trade a Krispy Kreme doughnut for a vegetable, or another episode of something on Netflix for a good night's rest.

If you and I are going to make it through this hard journey without the smell of smoke, we will likely need to make some intentional trades. As we cope, grieve, and heal, now may not be the wisest time to make gigantic trades. And we certainly don't need another item on our 'to do' list. While we cannot deny our reality or pretend it doesn't exist, there are times we could use a pause to make our days a smidge happier and healing a bit healthier.

We may each have different swaps we want or need to make. Honestly, I'd rather not trade a doughnut for broccoli, but maybe you do. One thing is for certain, we want our trades to move us forward on the road toward healing.

Before swapping begins, we have one limitation we should acknowledge. You and I can only trade what we have control over. I know. Sour attitudes and grumpy personalities of other people would make for a great trade. Unfortunately, that's not ours to trade.

While you think about exchanges you'd like to make, I'll mention a few.

Since laughter is already on the table, how about we trade our tears of sorrow for tears of laughter? I know it sounds impossible to think about laughing when life seems out of control. You might even feel guilty laughing.

Let's make a case for laughter. Maybe I don't need to. Most of us enjoy a good chuckle. But why? Laughter releases chemicals in our brains that relax the body. Laughter also causes us to breathe deeply, a proven technique for managing anxiety. And for all you exercisers out there, laughter is even exercise. Laughing can lighten the load of anger and impact our bodies in a host of healthy ways.

In our search for laughter, we don't have to limit our source of giggles to TV watching. You may have a friend, preferably female, with a great sense of humor. A fifteen-minute chat with her once a week might relieve your burdens for a few minutes.

Pets also are good for laughs. How about a little people watching? And children say the wildest things. Listen for people laughing when you go grocery shopping. Join them, from a distance lest they think you're strange. Read the comics. Play games. Take funny pictures of yourself. There are plenty of apps and filters for that.

Follow funny people on social media. Find a source of wholesome jokes. Try something new, the clumsier the better. Dance. Watch YouTube videos. Nowadays, I stay up too late watching videos by Christian comedian Tim Hawkins.

Some of these ideas require more effort than others. Try something that matches your energy level. That's why we chose TV. Subscribing to a meme channel might be the tickle your funny bone needs. Seek out small ways for the tears that leak from our eyes to come from laughter instead of sorrow.

With a little laughter on our lips, let's move on to another possible trade. Long before pornography shook up my world, I had a method of coping that had served me well for years. When something hard surfaced in life, I was quick to minimize my pain because somebody always had it worse. That is a true statement. Noble even.

We see hardships all around our world, even around the corner. Women suffer in dire circumstances and situations more challenging than our own. Reminding myself about the pain of others seemed like a healthy way to cope. Maybe you do the same thing. It can be good to have perspective.

But just because our pain doesn't appear more severe or tragic as someone else's, doesn't mean it doesn't hurt. We don't need to dwell on our heartache, but we do need to acknowledge our pain is just that, painful. I had to trade minimizing for acknowledging.

When we minimize what breaks our hearts, we avoid pain. Some might call that denial. *Drats.* I thought I was doing something healthy. Minimizing is a means of coping, which isn't bad. But we can't stay there. Coping is a stop on the road to healing. Just a stop. Not the destination.

When we minimize our pain, we can easily talk ourselves out of seeking help. Afterall, our situation isn't that bad. Sweeping our hurt under the proverbial rug won't serve us well in the long run. It would be easy for you and me to stoically say we're fine and wake up one day to find ourselves consumed with bitterness. We would simply be trading our heartache for bitterness. That's not the kind of trade we want to make.

Minimizing our hurt makes us appear strong and self-reliant. People may even comment on our strength. Our strength might be legit, or it could be the outer façade of minimized pain. Acknowledging and dealing with our hurts may bring tears, but it will also bring healing.

Perhaps you're on the other end of the spectrum where another person's pain couldn't possibly hurt more than yours. You are more alone, more desperate, and more unloved. We may perceive another person's life as easier but that doesn't mean it's true. Labeling pain on a scale from bad to unbearable for the sake of comparison doesn't do us any favors.

When we move into acknowledging our heartbreaks, we move away from minimizing and comparing. When it comes to personal pain, there is no competition. God calls us to compassion not comparison. We are called to share our burdens, not compare our burdens.

When I traded minimizing for acknowledgement, the pain came. I'll not lie to you, it hurt. What also came was healing. We need to feel our pain to heal our pain. This realization was pivotal in my healing. I hope it will be pivotal in yours too.

Okay, one more trade.

Does it annoy you when your people load the dishwasher wrong? For the millionth time, the cups go on top. Have you ever rolled your eyes when you walk in the bathroom to find the toilet paper roll going the wrong way on the holder? The right way is over not under. And we've all been irked by slow cashiers at the grocery store.

Over the course of the last few years, I realized I am easily and chronically offended. I frequently found myself annoyed over the smallest things. When I'm offended, it's a sure sign that kindness is taking a vacation. So, I've had to trade my right to be offended for kindness.

I'm not talking about being offended by our husband's pornography use. We should absolutely be offended by that and establish a zero-tolerance policy for pornography in our relationship. I'm talking about day-to-day occurrences that ruffle our feathers.

When we feel insulted when others don't see things the way we do, when traffic is slower than we anticipated, or we feel disrespected, offendedness can rear its head. When our feathers are ruffled, some external sign that lets people know we're not thrilled often follows. An eyeroll here, a condescending voice there, a cold shoulder. At least I found that to be true for me. Offendedness is often followed by a lack of kindness. Philippians 4:5 says to let your gentleness be evident to all. Sometimes mine isn't evident at all.

Maybe you don't show outward signs of annoyance at the time, but it simmers beneath the surface waiting for the right time to come out. Intentional lateness, stubbornness, disagreeable attitude, or procrastinating when others want you to do something. Passive aggressiveness is still unkindness. It just seems kinder because it's passive.

When we feel irritation rising in us, what if we choose to trade annoyance for niceness? That probably seems like a tall order because you're annoyed most minutes of most days. Living annoyed is exhausting. In Brant Hansen's book, *Unoffendable*, he says that being offended is tiring business. Letting things go gives us energy. Sounds weird, but I have found that to be true.

To give our energy level a boost, let's try offering a please and thank you to someone today. That's still a simple way to show kindness.

Those are some of my trades. Did any come to mind for you? You could trade those cozy pajamas for a pair of jeans. Or a box of tissues for a bike ride. But please don't beat yourself up if you're not ready for Levi's or spin class. Any small healthy trade is a small healthy step toward healing.

Even Jesus was a trade-er. He traded time in the spotlight for time with His Father. He traded the approval of men for the approval of His Father. He chose silence over justifying Himself. He traded His will for

God's will. And He traded the grandeur of heaven for a lowly earthly body.

We may not be able to trade our bodies in for a heavenly body yet, but we can be a trade-er just like Jesus. As you consider some trades you'd like to make, ask God to bring to mind some simple trades that would make your life more manageable, dare I say happier. If you're looking for a little dose of happy, *America's Funniest Home Videos* is always a good choice.

Laughter is an instant vacation.

— MILTON BERLE

A CALL TO COURAGE

It's helpful, and courageous, to recognize healthy and unhealthy areas in our lives. Awareness helps us know if a trade is needed. At a weekend intensive for spouses of sex addicts, I learned a valuable tool to keep me on track and moving forward. The three circles exercise can help you put specific things on paper to keep you moving in the right direction.

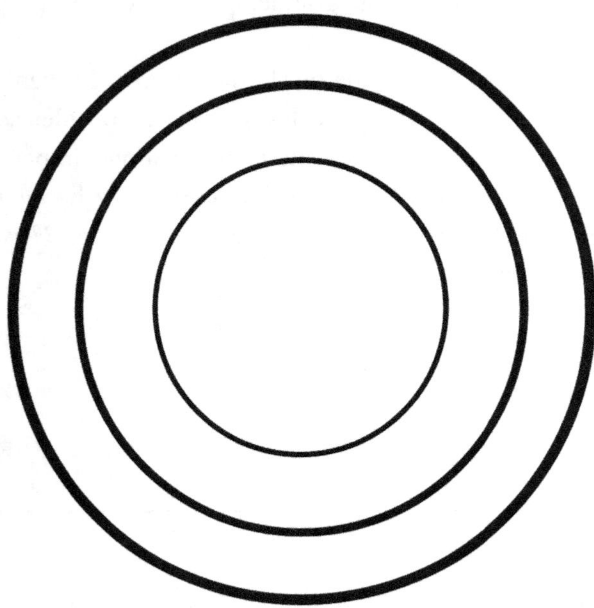

In the larger, outer circle write down healthy activities that keep you sane. Playing games, listening to music, taking a walk. Whatever floats your healthy boat. List as many things as possible. This is the circle we want to live in. It is spacious with room for options.

The middle circle is a caution circle filled with things that have the potential to throw us off-track. Include things here that would alert you to danger ahead. A big one for me is a lack of sleep or food. Hangry is real.

Last is the inner circle. In many areas of our life, we want to be in the inner circle, but not this one. This is the danger zone. Write down things that are unhealthy for you. Obsessively searching for evidence, apathy, avoidance. We don't want to camp here. When we realize we're here, we need to make a trade. Quickly!

Here is an example of how I completed my circle:

OUTER CIRCLE:

- Flexibility in schedule

- Eat healthy
- Quiet times most days
- Structured friendship building time with husband
- Write poems or anything
- Play safe games on iPad
- Read for fun
- Play games with children
- Listen to music
- Personal and corporate worship
- Massage, facial
- Time alone (home and away)
- Spend time with friends
- Journal
- Meeting with counselor
- Sleep 7-7.5 hours per night
- Limit sugar intake
- Exercise

MIDDLE CIRCLE

- House a wreck
- Not getting heart rate up through exercise
- Missing quiet times
- Too busy
- Stressed
- Fatigue
- Unhealthy eating
- Lack of sleep
- Hungry
- Isolation
- Media overload

INNER CIRCLE

- Apathy

- Avoidance
- Constantly searching for evidence of more porn use
- Skipping counseling sessions
- Saying critical things about husband to children
- Isolation

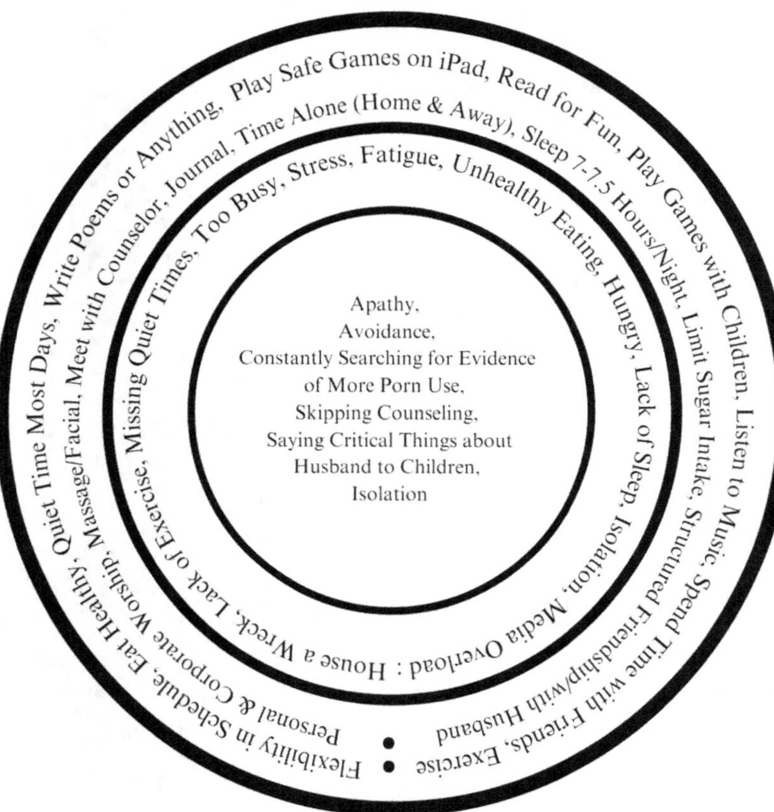

Chapter Nineteen

WHAT ABOUT MY CHILDREN?

Praise be to the God and Father of our Lord Jesus Christ, the Father of compassion and the God of all comfort, who comforts us in all our troubles, so that we can comfort those in any trouble with the comfort we ourselves receive from God. For just as we share abundantly in the sufferings of Christ, so also our comfort abounds through Christ.
2 Corinthians 1:3-5

Do you have a fun bedtime routine with your kids? Maybe you snuggle up on the couch with a good book or sing songs at the top of your lungs. When my kids were little, we had the best bedtime routine. It started when they were just wee tikes and went through elementary school.

We would start the bedtime process by reading a story. Or five. Sam is an avid reader and a great storyteller. He could ham up any book like nobody's business. Of course, it wasn't conducive for preparing for sleep, but it was fun, nonetheless.

After reading, we went around the room and everybody said something they were thankful for that day. It could be anything. A playdate, no homework, a good episode of *Clifford* (although I think they're all good), or a yummy meal. The latter was not likely at our house. I'm not a big fan of cooking, but they seem to want to eat, so I cook.

After a round of thankfulness, we would pray. Sometimes we'd all pray or just one of us. It depended on how late it was.

Some nights the bedtime routine would drag on longer than a tired mom had planned. Eight o'clock couldn't come fast enough because some nights you don't really care about the mouse getting a cookie or saying good night to the moon.

After we prayed, we would end our night with two questions followed by two declarations:

Parents: "What team are we on?"

Children: "The Allen Team."

Parents: "What do we do?"

Children: "Stick together in all kinds of weather."

And that's how our children went to bed most nights. Knowing we were a team that stuck together in all kinds of weather.

But then something happened. The weather changed, and the team started to fall apart. The weather didn't just change. Pornography addiction came in like a tornado and hovered over our family for years, ripping apart trust, raining down lies, and destroying the team that had so often prayed together. The Allen Team. Our family.

Even as the tornado was spinning, the facade was still intact, and life seemed normal to Bennett and Grace. They had married parents, few cares in the world, and a dog to love on after school.

For years, the tornado of pornography appeared to only affect our marriage, but Sunday came. Sunday was the day after Sam moved out. That's the day the tornado that had wreaked havoc on our marriage tore into Bennett and Grace's happy existence. The day the Allen Team fell apart.

Bennett and Grace had been at my aunt's house that weekend. They came home on Sunday ecstatic about the weekend with cousins. Sam worked that Sunday to make extra money but came over after work. We ate supper together like usual. Then it was time. Time for the whirlwind that had been destroying our marriage to crash into their sweet, innocent lives.

After supper we shuffled the ten steps to the living room dreading what was coming. Sam started the conversation. He assured them we loved them, that they had done nothing wrong, and nothing was their fault. He owned up to hurting me and said, "You know how we have told you that there are consequences to sin? I have made some bad choices and as a result of that I can no longer live here."

At first there was silence. Confusion swept across their faces. They looked at me hoping for clarification. My face confirmed the devastating news they had just heard. Then silence turned into sobs, loud gut-wrenching sobs. Sobs that a mom never wants to hear from her children. The aching of their hearts poured down their faces like a gushing river. They wept for a solid forty-five minutes.

This heartbreaking moment marked the saddest day in the life of our family. We had gone from praying together as the Allen Team to a fractured, sobbing mess.

I tried to hold back my emotions to be strong for Bennett and Grace, but the tears flowed like a stream down my cheeks too. I felt helpless. I wanted to protect them from this pain. I wanted to fix it and make it all better. But there was no sugarcoating reality: Daddy would not be living with us. Maybe ever again.

How confusing for a ten-year-old to go from a team that sticks together in all kinds of weather to a team that doesn't even live in the same house. Honestly, it was confusing for me.

Why in the world did God let it play out this way? He has the power to stop it all. He is pro marriage and wants families to stay together. Sure, I know God is sovereign and He can work all things together for the good of those who love Him (Romans 8:28), but, good grief, surely there is another way.

Between their sobs they asked. What did you do? Who said you can't live here?

What did he do? That's a loaded question. The angry and selfish part of me wanted to tell them about all the deception, rejection, and dismissal. How pornography had invaded our family and robbed us of the beautiful family we dreamed of on our wedding day. But the loving, nurturing part of me didn't want to shatter their hearts. The consequences spoke louder than my words ever could.

Sam answered the question as delicately and age appropriately as possible. But then there was the question, "Who said you can't live here?" I expected the "what did you do" question but not this one.

Now, not just his choices were on display but so were mine. While I felt confident in the decision I had made, I was, in fact, the one who said he could no longer live in our house.

Telling Bennett and Grace that he had hurt me immediately cast me in the victim role. Yes, I was a victim, but it also put me in the position to just forgive and go on like normal. Because that's what we teach our kids, to forgive. That's what God calls us to do. Forgive. That's what He does for us. Forgive. And if I didn't forgive, then it was my fault that he couldn't live with us.

In their innocent minds if he just said he was sorry and never did it again then things would be fine, and we could go on like normal. What they didn't know is that we had, in fact, done that more than once. They didn't know that forgiveness is not the same as trust. Saying sorry and promising never to look at pornography again wasn't an option anymore.

After lots of weeping Sam left and I was left with two distraught children. One sobbing uncontrollably and the other so angry they stormed out the front door into the darkness. I'm not ashamed to tell you that I had no idea what to do. None. I had never been to or heard of a parenting class that teaches you how to help your children manage their broken hearts so we managed as best we could.

That night our bedtime routine was far from fun and much, much different than in years past when we happily said what we were thankful for. That bedtime was dripping with tears and filled with uncertainty.

I still struggle a lot of days even now as I write these words. I really want to ask my kids those same bedtime questions and hear them declare, "Stick together in all kinds of weather." But the landscape of our family has changed. Things have been tossed and shifted and blown about until things are different.

Jesus was no stranger to being tossed around. Remember the story about Jesus on the lake with his disciples and a big storm popped up?

> Then he got into the boat and his disciples followed him. Suddenly a furious storm came up on the lake, so that the waves swept over the boat. But Jesus was sleeping. The disciples went and woke him, saying, "Lord, save us! We're going to drown!"
>
> He replied, "You of little faith, why are you so afraid?" Then he got up and rebuked the winds and the waves, and it was completely calm.
>
> The men were amazed and asked, "What kind of man is this? Even the winds and the waves obey him!"
>
> *Matthew 8:23-27*

I've never been on a boat during a storm, but I imagine there were some green faces, a bit of vomit, and a whole lot of panic while they frantically tried to keep the boat from sinking. Their boat rose and fell while the waves crashed around them.

The waves of your husband's pornography use are sweeping over you and your family. You may feel sick from the upheaval or feel like you're drowning in your tears. You might cry out, "Lord, save us! Lord, shield our children from the pain of separation, financial hardship, strained relationships, and the evils of the world we live in."

Just as God revealed himself to the disciples in a storm-tossed boat, He can use this hardship to reveal himself to our kids. When a need is exceeded or a card arrives or people help, those aren't just for our peace of mind and for us to experience God. They are opportunities for our children to experience God too. Invite your children into what God is doing, how He is meeting needs, showing kindness, and performing miracles.

So, when the question on the lips of the disciples pops up in the mouths of our children, "What kind of man is this?" they'll have experience with the God who walked them through the winds of family turmoil. They'll be familiar with the One who calms storms and heals broken people. Jesus won't just be someone we talk about. They'll know the miracle-working power of the God we sing about on Sunday mornings and pray to at bedtime.

When we read the story of the Jesus calming the storm, we want that to be our story. We want Jesus to speak to the whirlwind tossing around our lives and the lives of our children and make it stop. Who wouldn't want that? Whether Jesus chooses to calm the storm or not, one thing is certain, Jesus took care of His people, and He will take care of your people too. It may look different than we think it should. But His love for our children exceeds the love we feel for them, even on our best days.

Yes, we'd like our story to be different. We'd like our story to be like the bedtime stories we read to our children. They had predictable, happy endings.

You and I may not be able to predict our ending, but we can choose whether we live happily ever after.

Parenthood, the scariest hood you'll ever go through.

— AUTHOR UNKNOWN

A CALL TO COURAGE

Children spell love T-I-M-E. Engage your children for twenty minutes today. Get ice cream, take a walk, talk about whatever they want to talk about, answer their questions, paint something together, read together, have lunch, play a game, watch a movie. Anything. Just give them the time they desperately want.

It will be worth every exhausting minute.

Chapter Twenty

PARENTING WITH A NEW PERSPECTIVE

These commandments that I give you today are to be on your hearts. Impress them on your children. Talk about them when you sit at home and when you walk along the road, when you lie down and when you get up.
Deuteronomy 6:6-7

Because of our family's run-in with pornography, I am highly sensitive to pictures, TV shows, or movies that show a lot of skin. Maybe you are too. Our lives are different because of the road we've walked. And I parent differently for the same reason.

Several months after Sam moved out, my kiddos and I hopped on I-85 to run errands. What all fourth graders love to do with their free time. As soon as we merged onto the interstate a billboard caught my eye. Well, I'm sure it caught a lot of eyes. The billboard was advertising breast augmentation, but they didn't just use words. They used a picture of a woman's chest clothed in an itsy, bitsy, teeny, weeny bathing suit top. I'm not sure if was yellow polka dotted. There wasn't much of it. I didn't realize we'd have to sensor our drive to buy shoes.

As pornography infiltrates our homes and our highways, we are forced into conversations we'd rather not have, at least not while running errands. The entrance of pornography in our family has caused me to parent my children is a way that may be different than other parents. I'm okay with that.

Google says age eleven is the average age a child gets a cell phone. Age twelve is the average age a kid is exposed to pornography. It doesn't take a rocket scientist to connect the dots between cell phone use and pornography exposure. Access to pornography exposes children to things little minds and hearts are not prepared to handle.

When screens become the norm, it increases the urgency of talking to our kids about pornography. Long gone are the days when magazines and video stores were the only avenues for porn. It's available anywhere at any time to anybody. According to the U.S. Department of Justice, "Never before in the history of telecommunications media in the United States has so much indecent (and obscene) material been so easily accessible by so many minors in so many American homes with so few restrictions."

My children were late bloomers when it came to cell phones. They were twelve when their lives intersected with little rectangles. We did not give them shiny new phones. I'm too cheap for that. My friend Stephanie has a drawer full of old cell phones. She probably still does if you need one. She gave us two phones. My kids were thrilled with any phone. Of course, now they want the latest iPhone. I tell them to take a number, so do I.

Before we gave them cell phones, we had a family meeting to discuss expectations and guidelines of owning and using a cellphone. Even though Sam and I were separated and moving toward divorce, we all met together. He had experienced what a lifetime of pornography can do to a person, so guarding their eyes and their hearts was top priority.

First up on the cell phone agenda, they could have no expectation of privacy with their phones. I feel having birthed, raised, and paid for these children gives me the right to access to their phones. Not only is it my right as a parent, but it is also my responsibility to teach them about authority, accountability, and consequences.

I monitored their phones until sometime in high school. I didn't check their phones because I'm nosy but because I care. Well, maybe I am nosy, but I'm nosy because I care how they spend their time, what their eyes are consuming and who their friends are. To me, checking their phones is not an invasion of their privacy, it's an investment into their potential. The potential to live a life that brings glory to their Creator and good to a world that desperately needs it.

Besides, we paid for them. Well, technically Stephanie paid for the phones, but we are still paying the bill every month.

We also used a cell phone contract. I wish I could say I came up with this brilliant idea, but I did not. I found the contract in *Tech Savvy Parenting* by Brian Housman. The four of us sat and went over every point in the contract. My favorite: "I agree that if I am asked to turn off/hand over my phone and don't do so in a reasonable amount of time, the phone could be torched, destroyed, donated, etc." Each point was discussed and initialed by Bennett and Grace. Sam and I signed and dated the contract and put it on the refrigerator.

Of course, our goal wasn't to keep our children off their phones, although some days it felt like that. Our goal was to teach our children how to use their phones not their phones use them. Cell phones can be useful tools to manage life. I'd be lost without reminders on my phone. They can also be a powerful tool the enemy uses to tempt us to make poor choices or distract us from the people in the room.

I'm certainly not poo-pooing cell phones. I love mine. And I hate it. Every Sunday when I get the screen time usage report I cringe if it shows my screen time usage has gone up. I tell myself it is because I use it for work. And I do. But I can get sucked in like the next gal.

What I really want my kids to know is they have a choice. Not just in how they use their phones but how they manage their lives. They have a choice in the kind of person they want to be. Since they were captive to the car rider line for a lot of years, it was a good time to remind them of a thing or two.

When Bennett and Grace were in elementary school, we started something that we continued until they drove themselves to school. Before they stepped out of the car at school this was our exchange:

Me: "What are you?"

Them: "A child of God and an Allen."

Me: "What do you do?"

Them: "Make choices based on who I am."

I wanted to remind them they have a choice—in the person they are and the person they will become. Prior to our mantra, I prayed scriptures over them. I started with one verse in elementary school then realized middle school called for a different verse entirely. And high school needed a verse that would carry them into adulthood. Some mornings I speed prayed these verses, but I figure a speedy truth is better than no truth.

Elementary School

Satisfy us in the morning with your unfailing love,
that we may sing for joy and be glad all our days.
Psalm 90:14

Middle School

And the peace of God, which transcends all understanding,
will guard your hearts and your minds in Christ Jesus.
Philippians 4:7

High School

"The most important one," answered Jesus, "is this: 'Hear, O Israel: The Lord our God, the Lord is one. Love the Lord your God with all your heart and with all your soul and with all your mind and with all your strength.' The second is this: 'Love your neighbor as yourself.' There is no commandment greater than these."
Mark 12:29-31

Through Scripture, I wanted to turn their heart toward God,

because we may have some control over what is on their phone, but we have no control over what is on their friend's phone. Ultimately, they are responsible for what their eyes see.

I wish I could say I am super diligent and always on top of things. That I fervently pray for my kids. Some days I do. Some days, sadly, I forget to pray for my kids altogether.

Being a semi-responsible parent can be overwhelming especially if we're already in crisis mode. Everything seems daunting when our heart is aching. The last thing we want is to pile on more obligation or responsibility. We don't need more on our to-do list.

When I feel overwhelmed with mom responsibilities, I remind myself of one thing: God's grace is sufficient.

> But he said to me, 'My grace is sufficient for you, for my power is made perfect in weakness.' Therefore I will boast all the more gladly about my weaknesses, so that Christ's power may rest on me.
> *2 Corinthians 12:9*

When I mess up, I remind myself to do the best I can, and trust God will take care of the rest. He can use my weaknesses even if I don't understand how all that works. That frees me from the pressure to be a perfect mom. I don't know about you, but I'm relieved about that.

As we let out a huge sigh of relief from the expectations of being the perfect mom, our kids gladly let out their sigh of relief to know they don't have to be perfect kids. Just as we mess up, so do our kids.

I'm not suggesting we lower the standards, but just as we cut ourselves slack maybe we could do the same for our children. I am not the person to talk about this topic. I have high expectations for my kids and often apologize a lot for looking at their faults instead of their successes. But I do know it's true that our children deserve grace just as much as we do.

When we come to a bump in the road at our house, I admit that I have never been the mom of a nineteen-year-old before, and I have no idea what I'm doing. Likewise, they have never been a nineteen-year-old before, so we do the best we can to figure it out together.

One of many things I have not been able to figure out is how to shield my children from the pain of addiction and divorce. I would like to wrap them up like I did when they were babies, burrito style, and keep them from everything that hurts. I expect they would have some objection to burrito-style parenting as a teenager, so I have to let them experience the pain as it comes their way. Just as God works all things together for my good, He works all things together for their good too.

God is using their pain just like He is using my pain. Their experience with pornography addiction in our family might be the very thing that gives them courage to turn their heads when they see objectional billboards on the highway. That helps me see things from a different perspective.

> I'm at a point in my parenting where "What did I just say?!" could either be a threat or a genuine question.
>
> — UNKNOWN AUTHOR

A CALL TO COURAGE

Now is the time to start a conversation with your children about pornography. Include pornography in conversations about finances, sex, navigating relationships, and faith.

Pornography is a huge part of our culture, so putting our head in the sand won't make it go away. You and I know that better than anyone. Put a date on the calendar and start conversations with your children. You might be shocked at what they already know.

The following are some practical ideas to help minimize exposure to pornography:

- Check your kid's phone and social media accounts until you feel comfortable with their decision-making skills.
- Know their friends.
- Set up guidelines for cell phone use. Try a cell phone contract. You can find examples online.
- Put computers in open areas so the screen is visible.
- Use parental controls, install a filter on computers, phones, tablets, anything that has access to the internet.
- Keep screens out of bedrooms and bathrooms.
- Keep phones downstairs or in common areas.
- Engage your children, age appropriately and God honoring, regarding what is happening in your family. They'll want to hear it from you, not somebody else.
- Keep the lines of communication open.

Helpful reminders for our kids:

- God loves you. He is not out to ruin your fun. His boundaries are for your protection.
- It's never too late to start over.
- Possessing sexually explicit pictures of minors is illegal.
- Hidden apps aren't hidden from God.
- Choosing who we live life with can affect our future.
- Future employers look at social media accounts.
- It's okay to block numbers, but not those of parents.
- Parents are on your side.
- Honesty really is the best policy.

Chapter Twenty-One

LET IT GO

Be kind and compassionate to one another, forgiving
each other, just as in Christ God forgave you.
Ephesians 4:32

I have spent my share of time in counseling shedding buckets of tears, digging deep into my hurting heart, and using countless tissues. We have prayed, talked past our time limit, and cried some more. Rarely did I leave a counseling session thinking this was the session that really helped me. Rather, as one session built on another, we talked through the hurt and uncovered insecurities. There was no zapping away the pain or solving my problems in one fifty-minute session.

I admit that it would be nice to go to counseling and it be a one and done deal. Unfortunately, that's not how the human heart works. At least, that's not how my heart works.

There was, however, one session that stands out. One session that freed me in ways I didn't know I needed to be freed. God is gracious to give us things we don't know we need.

I spent many sessions trying to understand why things were the way they were. Why would a rational person choose to do things that seem so irrational and risk everything dear to them? I just couldn't make sense of it. You might be feeling the same way. Perhaps you're wondering why your husband is throwing away his future with his family for some pictures on a screen. It makes no sense.

During one of our sessions, my counselor said the most freeing thing, and I hope you find it freeing as well. She said, "You are not an addict so you will never think like an addict. Let it go."

Let. It. Go.

I had no idea how much I needed to hear that. A weight lifted off my shoulders. She didn't mean to let go of my marriage or let go of my standards or the things necessary to reestablish trust. Or to condone or accept pornography in my marriage. She meant to let go of my incessant need to figure things out. I'm an overthinker. In my quest to understand, I found myself wrapped up in reasoning things that couldn't be reasoned. And I was stuck.

My movement forward in healing went at a snail's pace. I kept waiting for him to be or do something in his recovery so that I could move forward in mine. I was unknowingly making my healing dependent upon his. When I decided to let go, I finally started moving forward.

This realization didn't change our circumstances, but it changed me. I learned to release what didn't make sense and stop trying to figure out why he thought this or did that. I had to let go of my need to control his behavior or thoughts or eye gaze.

Maybe you have some things you need to let go of too. You will need courage to let go because letting go can be hard. It is retraining, reframing, and rethinking. Letting go is choosing not to think about or engage in things you can do nothing about. And that is freeing because you don't have to try to make sense of the senseless or figure out why someone said this or did that.

Letting go paved the road of healing for me. A road marked with baby steps of forgiveness is:

- A deliberate decision to let go.
- Letting go of resentment and choosing not to hold a grudge.

- Letting go of something painful and hard so you can take hold of something freeing and life-giving.
- Choosing to no longer hold onto pain and disappointment.
- Choosing to let God's loving and nail-scarred hands hold it for you.
- The way forward.

Forgiveness is not based on whether a person deserves it or not. Letting go is not saying what a person did is right, okay, or acceptable. When we forgive, we're not saying I trust you nor does it mean you are suddenly okay, or the relationship is restored.

And forgiveness is not fair. That doesn't sound very spiritual, but it's true. Forgiveness is a lot of things, but fairness is not one of them.

When we've been wronged, we feel like it's our right to hold a grudge. I mean, he has been looking at pornography, ripping out our heart, and dismissing our feelings. We feel justified in holding something against him. At least I did.

By holding a well-deserved grudge, it feels like we're somehow winning, like we have the upper hand. It's just that the hand we're holding isn't a winning hand.

As you know, I am a gal who likes to play games, but I am also a gal who likes to win games. I have a bit of a competitive streak buried somewhere inside me, likely lodged somewhere between my love for peanut butter and my dislike for cooking. I was never the mom to let my kids win at games unless it was Monopoly because someone had to stop the torture.

Since I'm a tad on the competitive side, I think about forgiveness in those terms. Here is the deal breaker for me: When you and I choose not to forgive, we lose twice.

The first loss happens when we are sucker punched by our husband's disclosure, or by finding pornographic pictures, or how ever we found out about our husband's pornography problem. It is by no means a win for the husbands, but it's certainly a mark in the loss column for us.

The second loss happens when we choose to hold onto bitterness or nurse a grudge. When we cling to resentment or our right to be right, we live in defeat. It may not feel like defeat at the time, of course, but as the pages tear off the calendar, resentment tears away our kindness, our joy, and our freedom leaving us older, more bitter, and maybe even a little mean.

We can choose a different way, a better way. We have the freedom to choose. We can choose if we want to be the kind of woman who takes God at His Word. You see, we can't hold tightly to grudges or bitterness and have an open hand to receive what God wants to give us. God doesn't force open our hand. We get to decide if the tradeoff is worth it. You'll be glad to know it's not an even trade. God always gives more than we give up.

It can seem like we're giving up so much. It may even seem like we're giving up more than the person who hurt us. Honestly, we are giving up a lot. We're giving up anger, hatefulness, bitterness, our right to be right, and our desire to get even. We are giving up things that are holding us back from living free.

Since I prefer winning, I choose forgiveness when hatefulness creeps in or when "that serves you right" finds its way to my lips. While forgiveness isn't fair, forgiving is winning. That is good news for us competitive girls.

Forgiveness isn't fair, but it is freeing. Beth Moore puts it like this, "The brutal irony of unforgiveness is, it keeps us bound to the very people we most want to be free of. They are roped to our backs and go everywhere we go. Forgiveness is not a feeling. It's a freedom. It's coming into agreement with God to cut them loose and put them in His hands."

Do you want to be free? To stop reliving the past and start living in the present. If so, you and I have a choice to make. You can keep holding onto unforgiveness or you can let it go and live free. But you can't do both.

Forgiveness wasn't fair for Jesus either. He died on a cross for sins He didn't commit so that you and I could be forgiven for sins we did commit. There's nothing fair about that.

The Bible says that every single one of us has sinned and fallen short of God's standard. That means we're all in need of the forgiveness Jesus died for. We're all in need of someone to save us from our sins.

Maybe you don't know you need a Savior because you're a pretty good person. You haven't robbed a bank or taken the life of another. But maybe, like me, you have robbed someone of joy because your words have been harsh or critical. Or, like me, you haven't taken another person's life, but you've taken advantage of another person's kindness.

Every person on this planet needs a Savior. But Jesus didn't just die to save us from our sins so we can live with Him forever sometime out in the future. He did do that, but He also died to save us from ourselves so we can live every day with Him right now, which is only possible when we acknowledge our need for forgiveness.

While we are considering forgiveness for our husbands, let's consider our need for forgiveness. Forgiveness for our sins. Outbursts of anger, little white lies, binge shopping, or eating. The God of the universe died so that you and I can live free from these things. Free from harsh words, gossip, and unkind thoughts.

His death on the cross was personal. He died for you. Will you accept His gracious gift? Will you acknowledge your sins and realize your need for a Savior? Will you choose Jesus to be your Forgiver and Leader of your life? He would be so pleased by your surrender.

Maybe you already know Jesus, but you're not sure if you're stuck in unforgiveness or not. Sometimes we invite unforgiveness in and happily give it a home. Other times unforgiveness sneaks in and takes up residence and we don't realize it's happening.

Do any of these statements ring true for you? If so, unforgiveness may be eroding the freedom Jesus died to give you.*

1. You're experiencing outbursts of anger.
2. You're petty and impulsive.
3. You're desperate to make them understand how you feel.
4. You're compulsive.

---

* Cylon George, "Unforgiveness," *Spiritual Living for Busy People*, spirituallivingfor busypeople.com/unforgiveness, (accessed 11/22/24)

5. You're unable to reframe your experiences.
6. You're not taking responsibility for your feelings.
7. You're sick.
8. You're keeping a list of offenses.
9. You hate yourself.
10. You replay the scene over and over.
11. You gossip about them.
12. You're righteous and entitled.
13. You exercise poor judgement.
14. You refuse to confide in others.

I will admit that I have checked one or two or all of these at some point. I have replayed scenes over and over, perched myself above others in self-righteousness, and failed to take responsibility for my feelings. And the number of times I've blurted out angry words is sickening.

You may have noticed the word that each statement has in common. You. Each statement is about you, not your husband, your neighbor, or your kids.

If we are living life with a body of believers, we are frequently reminded that life isn't about us. If we have children, we remind them that the world doesn't revolve around them. But when it comes to forgiveness, it is about us. Forgiveness isn't about the other person.

Forgiveness is about me choosing, growing, and letting go. It really is about me.

As you inch your way forward in your dark tunnel fifty minutes at a time, I want to remind you of the three simple words that can bring you freedom: Let it go. You'll be glad you did.

> Forgiving someone may cost you your pride, but not forgiving them will cost you your freedom.
>
> — CHARLES F. GLASSMAN

A CALL TO COURAGE

Forgiveness is a journey that starts with a choice. Will you choose forgiveness? If so, say it out loud, write it on paper, write with lipstick on your mirror. Honestly answer the following questions to see if unforgiveness is holding you back. If you're not there yet, don't beat yourself up. Keep choosing forgiveness. Freedom waits on the other side.

1. Is the first thought you have about them the pain they caused in your life?
2. Would you help them if you knew they were in trouble and you had the ability?
3. Can you think positive thoughts about this person?
4. Do you still think of getting even? Does your heart want to hurt them?
5. Have you stopped looking for them to fail?

Chapter Twenty-Two

WHATEVER IT TAKES

> Trust in the LORD with all your heart
> and lean not on your own understanding.
> *Proverbs 3:5*

When we neared the point where separation was moving toward divorce, I found myself sobbing on my living room floor. Again. Weeping because things weren't going the way I had hoped. I had run out of things to pray for. I really wanted to ask God to do whatever it took to save my marriage, but I was too scared. I didn't have the courage to pray a prayer that bold and mean it.

As tears dripped into the carpet, a sermon from years past crept into my mind. Sometimes I can't remember a Sunday sermon by Wednesday but this one has stuck around for years. The sermon consisted of three simple truths that all Jesus-following people need to be sure of:

1. I can trust God.
2. He is good.

3. God loves me.

This trio of truths helped me understand my hesitancy in prayer and why apprehension was winning over boldness.

I can trust God. As I mulled over this truth, I realized I didn't wholeheartedly trust Him. I had just lived through two years of God showing up and doing neat things, but somewhere along the way doubt snuck in. When hope turned into hopelessness, doubt reared its head. I was torn between wanting to trust God and actually trusting Him.

I had already put my trust in counseling, a treatment center, and stacks of books, which are all great things. I had prayed everything I could think of. But asking God to do whatever it takes is scary when you're not sure the One you're surrendering to is trustworthy.

Trusting God is hard. We want to pray "Your will be done on earth as it is in heaven" and mean it. He puts air in our lungs every day, all day. The sound of His voice brought the world into existence. He's omnipotent, omnipresent, and omniscient. God is worthy of our trust.

When I examined my lack of trust, I realized I was basing my trust in God on what He did instead of who He is. If God didn't do this or that, then He must not be trustworthy. My trust was based on His performance. I had in my mind what I felt like a trustworthy God should do. Save marriages, restore families, heal people. He wasn't doing that.

The problem with performance-based trust is God doesn't always do what we want. Isaiah 55:8-9 says, "'For my thoughts are not your thoughts, neither are your ways my ways,' declares the LORD. 'As the heavens are higher than the earth, so are my ways higher than your ways and my thoughts than your thoughts.'"

Our trust in God can't be rooted in God doing what we think is best or right because His ways are different and higher than our ways. Of course, sometimes God answers our prayers with a big yes. But when the marriage ends, the prognosis is terminal, or the business fails, is God still trustworthy?

Author Jennifer Rothchild shared her wisdom about trusting God through a quote on Instagram: You don't have to understand God fully to be able to trust Him completely.

When we don't understand what God is doing, it doesn't mean He isn't trustworthy. When our circumstances don't make sense, we have a choice to make. We can believe what is true or what we feel like is true. The truth is that God is trustworthy.

With a better grasp of what it means to trust God, my mind wandered to our second truth. **God is good.**

Out of these three truths, this is the one I struggled with most. I wasn't convinced God is good. I feared if I asked Him to do whatever it took to save my marriage, something bad might happen. He might afflict my children with a disease or allow a car accident to happen to someone I love. I'm not saying that's good theology. That's how I felt. I was afraid God had His finger on the smite button waiting to do something drastic and terrible. I didn't trust He was good enough or kind enough to answer a prayer so raw and earnest.

It's hard to trust someone you're not sure is good. How do we grapple with human trafficking, child abuse, and other atrocities and still say God is good? How can we wake up day after day in our current circumstance and say God is good? When we feel rejected, financially devastated, or mistreated, how can we say God is good? I couldn't pray a prayer so bold because I wasn't sure God would be good in His answer.

Clearly the Bible states that God is good. I wholeheartedly believe God's Word is the absolute truth. So it is, in fact, true that He is good even if I don't understand it. Just as with trust, God can still be good and me not understand it. I can choose to believe it and operate knowing biblical facts are greater than my lack of understanding or fears.

The Bible not only declares God is good, but it also says He works all things together for our good. He can take difficult things and mix them with other hard things and make something good. Not just for our good but for the good of His kingdom.

It's God's process for purpose. It's like baking a cake. Oh, wait. Did I just make a cooking reference? In and of themselves, the ingredients are not that tasty, except maybe the sugar. But when you throw in flour, eggs, and other ingredients, you have the potential to create something good for yourself and to share with others. Although if you choose to eat the whole thing, there is no judgment from me.

He can take all the heartache and tears and use it for our good because He has a purpose for our pain. Suffering without purpose is pointless and cruel. Suffering with purpose is good, even when it's hard. It may seem like we are suffering without purpose, especially when things don't turn out that way we envisioned. But God's vision for our lives is not limited by our vision.

In Ken and Joni Eareckson Tada's book, *Joni and Ken*, they write, "There is no circumstance, no trouble, no testing that can ever touch me until, first of all, it has gone past God and past Christ, right through to me. If it has come that far, it has come with great purpose." God takes our circumstances, trouble and testing and uses them for our good, even when we don't like it or understand it.

I admit that walking the road of pornography addiction in my family and eventually divorce makes zero sense to me. I don't understand why my kids have endured the pain of divorce. I don't understand why pornography is such a massive money-making business. I don't understand why the world turns a blind eye to the destructive nature of pornography.

Fortunately, you and I don't have to understand for God to use our pain for good. We do have to choose to lean on His understanding instead of our own.

Noah probably didn't understand why he was building an ark with no rain in the forecast. If Noah had leaned on his own understanding, there would have been no ark. We can trust His character even when we don't understand His ways.

One last thing about God's goodness that challenged my thinking comes from Psalm 119:68a: "You are good and what you do is good."

God is not only good and uses all things for our good, but God does good things.

He breathes life into an infant and brings rain during drought. He heals broken bones, forgives sin, and creates laughter. I don't think we can dispute that God does good things. The issue is more of what He doesn't do. He doesn't stop production, consumption, and fallout of a world hooked on pornography.

It may seem God is passively standing by allowing tragedies, divorces, and deaths to happen endlessly. When trauma wrecks our world, we question God's care and His character. Sure, God does good things, but it's the presence of bad things that cause us to doubt.

When we question God's character, we don't stop to question our own, personally, and collectively as a human race. Genesis tells us that God created Adam and Eve and His creation was very good. Somewhere between creation being very good and the sewing together of fig leaves, badness slithered in in the form of a snake. Satan tricked Eve into eating fruit from the only tree in the whole garden that God said not to eat. Really, one tree? There were zillions of other trees, but Eve chose the lone tree God had forbidden. Right there in the middle of a perfect garden, bad choices were made, not by God but by humans.

When Eve chose to believe Satan over God, she was exercising the very thing a good God gave her. Choice. Eve leaned on her own understanding, what seemed right and good for her. When she chose fruit over the Fruit-Giver, paradise was lost. Eve got what she thought she wanted but lost what she had.

I would rather not associate myself with Eve, but we look too much alike. Unfortunately, we all resemble our first parents. The apple didn't fall far from the tree.

You and I may look like our first parents, but we don't have to choose to like them. Adam and Eve chose unwisely and blamed it on someone else. That does sound an awful lot like me sometimes. There is still a liar, cheater, and stealer seeking to trip us up, but we can wise up to a new way of choosing. We will never choose perfectly, but we can choose purposefully.

So, when the evening news reports a barrage of evil around the corner and around the world, we can be assured that a good God gave regular people the opportunity to choose. It is easy to point our finger at God and wonder why there is so much evil in the world.

There is evil in the world because God is good and gives us choices. He could wave His magic wand and make it all go away. Instead, Jesus stepped into the history books to fix what man had broken. A good God made a way for humanity to be restored.

It is His restoration that brings us to the last trio of truth. **God loves me.**

Love seems undefinable and vague. For humans, love is a commitment, but it's also feelings of affection, interest, or pleasure. We can love people, basketball, and leopard print.

When the style trends change, do we still love tie dyed, permed hair, and blue eyeshadow? I used to love exercise. Now, my bones creak and my knees ache which makes me love it less. At least that's what I'm tell myself for the reason I don't go to the gym much anymore.

As we know, feelings come and go. Love is no exception. The love we experience on our wedding day can fade by our fifth anniversary. Our hearts melt when we bring that cute puppy home, but when the whining keeps you awake, loves fades.

Our love holds grudges and retaliates. But God's love is not the same as our love. A defining feature of God's love is His steadfastness. God's love never changes or gets old. When it's winter, God loves us. When we blow it, God loves us. When we ________, God loves us.

God doesn't love us any less when we skip Bible study or attend Bedside Baptist. The fact is God loves us. Period.

John 3:16 says that God loves the world, a giant collection of people. But what about all the people in the world individually? What about me? The curly-headed girl living in North Carolina. What about you? Loving the masses is different than loving individuals.

Fortunately, God doesn't see crowds the way we see crowds. When crowds of people followed him in the Bible, He didn't just see a multitude of people looking for a miracle. He saw individuals in need of a Savior. He saw one person plus another person plus another person. And He sees you. You are not overlooked.

When you and I struggle to believe God loves us, it's possible our struggle isn't with God as much as it is with ourselves. Perhaps, we don't see ourselves as loveable. We can think of a million reasons why God doesn't or shouldn't love us. We're too needy, too inconsistent, or too bothersome. We forget to pray, struggle with depression, yell at our kids, eat too many cookies, or spend too much money. Or worse, all of them.

How could God love a person like that? We will never know how, but He does. Just because I don't feel like God loves me doesn't mean it isn't true. Again, our lack of understanding doesn't negate the truth.

A couple decades ago I was challenged with the issue of God's love for me. I flew halfway across the country to a women's retreat to spend four days at a camp in the middle of nowhere Colorado. I cried, made new friends, and left with this take away: God loves me.

While I don't understand the fact that God loves me, I do accept it as a fact. Some days I don't feel it or see it or live that way. When I forget that He loves me, my encounter with Jesus in the Rocky Mountains is my stake in the ground reminding me of His love for me.

Do you have a stake in the ground? Can you pinpoint a moment in time when you chose to believe God loves you? If not, take out your hammer, grab a stake, and pound it into the ground today. Even if you don't wholeheartedly believe it yet, let today be the day you choose to believe God loves you. Let today be the day you reflect on decades from now.

After lots of crying on my living room floor and mulling over these three truths, I hoisted my weary bones to the couch. I still didn't completely believe or understand these three truths, but I believed them enough to take a risk. So, I mustered the courage and blurted, "Lord, do whatever it takes to save my marriage."

> You cannot swim for new horizons until you have courage to lose sight of the shore.
>
> — WILLIAM FAULKNER

A CALL TO COURAGE

Trio of Truths: God loves me. I can trust Him. He is good.

Are these actual truths to you or just nice words you hear at church? Make them your truth. Put your stake in the ground. Decide today God is safe enough to ask Him to do whatever it takes.

Chapter Twenty-Three

GOOD GRIEF

The Lord is close to the brokenhearted
 and saves those who are crushed in spirit.
Psalm 34:18

In March 2020, the Covid-19 pandemic swept across the world. People were told to stay at home, the grocery store shelves were bare from panic buying, and all major league sports were halted. Even the Olympics were postponed. Schools were ordered closed, churches weren't meeting in person, people lost their jobs, and you couldn't find toilet paper anywhere. The whole world was instructed to socially distance to alleviate the spread of the coronavirus.

Perhaps you don't need the government to tell you to practice social distancing these days. Since you've found out about your husband's betrayal, you've been practicing your own form of social distancing. And understandably so.

Whatever reason for your social distancing the result can be the same. Loneliness. You may feel alone in a room filled with people. Or left out while scrolling through social media looking at happy marriage pictures when you're crying yourself to sleep because your husband is interested in pictures instead of you. Loneliness is that depressing feeling when you simply don't have company.

During the pandemic, I remember sitting alone at my kitchen table in my empty house with tears dripping from my eyes. I wasn't crying because I was panicking or didn't have food in my freezer. I had everything I needed, and we were healthy. I was crying because I was lonely. I had no one to share in the unknowns of a pandemic. I had no one to share in the great toilet paper hunt. And I had no one to talk to. I felt the loneliest I had ever felt in my life.

Sure, I had friends. But once you've experienced the everydayness and connection found in marriage, that severed connection, whether temporary or permanent, can lead to loneliness that feels lonelier during unusual or difficult times.

At times like these we are missing what Dr. Ned Hallowell calls the other Vitamin C. Connection. We all need connection, not just company. When we lack connection, our lives can be filled with people while our hearts are drained with loneliness.

Are you feeling lonely? Are you missing the connection you once had during long walks or quiet evenings in front of the TV? Or the togetherness of weekend getaways or date nights. If you're separated, you may miss having someone to help with the kids, run to the store to pick up the missing ingredient, or take care of you when you're sick. We have a lot to miss even if the relationship wasn't spectacular.

Loss is all around us and part of all our lives. Trees lose their leaves, dogs shed their winter coats, and us older folks lose our hair or at least the color. Loss simply means being without something we once had or dreamed of. You and I are grieving what we had or thought we had. We are grieving what we've lost.

With all this loss, how can we have hope? When we feel alone and overcome by our losses, hope can seem like an unattainable reality. Where is hope in our loneliness and our losses?

A day is coming when all the losses will stop, when all the tears, unfairness, and deception will end. The day when Jesus makes all things new. That is good news for some time in the future, but what does that mean today when the tears won't stop and our hearts ache from the pain of rejection? How can we find hope in our losses right now?

We don't have to wait until Jesus comes back to have hope. Our hope for today, for right now, can be summed up in one small but large sentence: God is faithful.

God keeps showing up in our lives, even when we don't recognize it. He shows up with every breath we breathe. He shows up when we see the colors of a sunset. He shows up when the birds sing, when we have money to pay our bills, and when we have strength to put one foot in front of the other. God consistently keeps showing up day after day.

But God is more than consistent. Yes, the Bible says God is the same yesterday, today, and tomorrow. I'm grateful for that. We could use some dependability in our lives. But faithfulness is more than dependability or consistency.

Faithfulness is about loyalty. Faithfulness is rooted in loyalty. God is loyal. He keeps showing up not because He has to, but because He wants to.

When we struggle through hard times, we may not recognize God's loyalty. We may be too dazed to notice that God is still working on our behalf. Or perhaps we've walked with God a long time and gotten used to His loyalty. His faithfulness may be old hat to us. Whatever the case, acknowledging God's faithfulness can bring hope when our circumstances seem bleak.

When the Israelites were set free from years of slavery, their disobedience sent them wandering in the desert for forty years. Because of God's loyalty to His people, He was with them every day while they traipsed through the wilderness. Every single day God provided a cloud to protect them from the harsh sun and fire for them to see at night. He didn't do that out of duty. He did it out of love.

When they got hungry, God fed them. He rained down manna from heaven for them to eat. I have no idea how the calendar worked back then, but for 312 days each year (no manna on the Sabbath) for forty years God served up food to the people He called His own. I'm not a mathematician, but that is 12,480 times that God provided manna.

The first time or perhaps even the first month manna came, they may have been awed by God's faithfulness to provide. But on year twenty-three and day 187, it's quite possible that they didn't think twice about God's faithfulness. Manna supernaturally appearing became old hat to them.

Even when they disobeyed, God fed them. When they grumbled and complained, God gave them food. And when they lost hope in ever making it to the Promised Land, God still gave them manna.

On their forty-year camping trip their clothes didn't wear out and their shoes didn't wear thin. God was faithful to them over and over again. He was loyal because He loved them. He was more than consistent in His actions. He was faithful with His love.

Do you see evidence of God's faithfulness in your life right now? Recognizing His faithfulness when our eyes are clouded with tears and our hearts are broken can be like looking through fog-covered glasses.

We may not see His faithfulness in this current trial, but His faithfulness may be apparent in other areas. For example, we may not see God working in our relationship right this second, but we may see Him moving in our finances or our health or in the lives of those we love.

When we can recognize His faithfulness in other areas, it shores up our faith in areas where we may not see so clearly. God is always working. All the time. Everywhere. In every circumstance.

Even amid God's faithfulness, we can still be sideswiped by our losses. Losses can appear out of nowhere. In his book, *Recovering from Losses in Life*, H. Norman Wright suggests that most of us go through life with ungrieved losses. One loss pile on top of another loss and we live a life laden with loss. We carry around a collection of losses we haven't taken time to acknowledge or grieve.

Typically, when loss happens, we pick ourselves up by our bootstraps and move on without taking time to grieve. For some losses like death, divorce, financial loss, or losing a friend we may take time to grieve or seek counsel. But there are other losses in our lives, such as sending a child to college, job changes, death of a dream, moving, and all sorts of "lesser" losses, that are swept under the rug because we're pushed on to the next thing. We may cry on the inside but never on the outside.

To help us grieve our losses, Dr. Wright recommends a process called a programmed cry, an intentional time set aside to cry and grieve loss. He suggests we grab a picture of a loss we need to grieve, go to a quiet, dim lit area, and turn on soft music. I'd throw in a box of tissues too.

He invites us to look at the picture and remember. Reflect on the good times and the bad. Express your fears, anger, disappointment, and frustration along with the happiness, contentment, and peace you once experienced. Say each out loud. Let the tears flow. Take time to stay in the emotion. Talk to God and let healing happen right there in the midst of your tears.

Since I'm game for a good cry and a fan of good emotional health, I decided to give it a try. I sat in my closet one day while the kids were at school with a lamp on the floor beside me and a family picture in hand. I remembered the joy of vacations, family dinners, and that spur-of-the-moment trip to the mountains to play in the snow. I reminisced about anniversary trips, Christmas shopping, and laughing with friends. I also remembered the emotional distance, going to bed alone, the deceit, and the shock as I sat in front of my computer. I recalled feeling out of control and helpless to change a situation I desperately wanted to be different. And I cried.

In the closet I grieved what I had lost. I lost a marriage that was once fun and fulfilling. I lost a family that took bikes rides together. I lost the excitement of Christmas morning as a family. I lost the connection that happens when two people share a life. I grieved losses that had accumulated over time.

The process wasn't long or drawn out. There was no magical formula. I remembered the pain, acknowledged the losses, and took a step toward healing.

The prophet Jeremiah wrote about remembering his losses in the book of Lamentations: "I remember my affliction and my wandering, the bitterness and the gall. I well remember them, and my soul is downcast within me. Yet this I call to mind and therefore I have hope: Because of the Lord's great love we are not consumed, for his compassions never fail. They are new every morning; great is your faithfulness" (Lamentations 3:19-23).

Jeremiah remembered the difficulties that weighed him down. He remembered the bitter struggles that made him feel lost. He also remembered God's love and faithfulness. In remembering God's faithfulness, he found hope. And it was God's day-in and day-out faithfulness that helped him rise from his despair.

That same faithfulness can bring us hope too. Every morning when our puffy eyes awake and our feet hit the floor, God is faithful. When someone we love is absent, unavailable, or unwilling, God is present, available, and willing. When our husbands are unfaithful, God is loyal.

Whether your lungs cry sobs in your closet, your shower or your kitchen table, the day is coming when God will wipe away every tear. In the meantime, God's loyalty is as daily as the sunrise. We can "hold unswervingly to the hope we profess, for he who promised is faithful" (Hebrews 10:23).

We can rest knowing that He will never leave us or forsake us. And He is never socially distant.

> One is the loneliest number.
>
> — THREE DOG NIGHT

A CALL TO COURAGE

Grab a picture, maybe a wedding picture or family picture, go to a private place and take time to grieve your loss. Remember, grieve, and heal.

Chapter Twenty-Four

INCHING BACK INTO LIFE

"Forget the former things;
  do not dwell on the past.
See, I am doing a new thing!
  Now it springs up; do you not perceive it?
I am making a way in the wilderness
  and streams in the wasteland."
Isaiah 43:18-19

The lights dimmed, the music started, and my heart raced in my chest. Insecurity gripped my insides, and I was a nervous wreck. What had I done? What in the world was I thinking? But it was too late. There was no turning back. The time had come for me to stop hiding.

This was the night I crawled out from underneath the rock of fear and shame. The night courage won. The night I publicly shared the story of how my husband's pornography use had changed my life. Four years had passed since that Saturday in September. Four hard, emotional, and painful years. And now was the time to courageously shout God's faithfulness from the rooftop. Well, a stage not a rooftop.

I wasn't a stranger to the stage. I took a drama class in high school three decades ago and had done some acting at church back in the day. The difference between those days and this day was someone else had written the script. Now I was the one who had written the words. Not only had I written the words, but I had also lived the words.

I meticulously typed out my notes, highlighting, underlining, and folding down the pages so they didn't stick together. I chose a gigantic font to compensate for the curse of old age. As I placed my notes on the podium and waited for the lights to come up, I surrendered to my reality. Not just my current reality of hundreds of women staring at me, but the reality that brought me to the stage.

Pornography created wounds where dreams had once been. Pornography ripped what should have been sewn and separated what should have been connected. Pornography had wrecked my marriage.

Part of that wreckage meant I needed a job. I confess that I wasn't eager to get a job after being a stay-at-home mom for ten years. After all, hanging out in yoga pants beats wearing makeup any day, but necessity trumped preference. We needed the money. With a mushy brain and a heart full of insecurities, I took a job at my church.

After a couple years on the job, our church needed a leader for our women's ministry. Since I was a woman and I was willing, I was the girl for the job. My job in women's ministry led me to the stage that night.

The night God unleashed a whole new way of thinking for me. I started to believe God really could do something good with my life. Maybe even something big.

My life had been tainted with shame and divorce, but that night God gave me a new perspective—the last few years weren't just painful years of misery, they were preparation for ministry. If I would cooperate, God could use my past to build my future. A good future.

In Genesis 50:20 Joseph told his brothers, "You intended to harm me, but God intended it for good to accomplish what is now being done, the saving of many lives." Joseph's brothers hated him and sold him into slavery, but God used Joseph's suffering for good to position him to save the lives of an entire population including his brothers.

You and I may not save an entire population from starvation, but

God can use the unthinkable in our lives to do the unfathomable. What Satan intended to tear us down, God can use to build our future.

God is always building, growing, and developing. Since pornography entered the picture, you and I have done our share of crying and fuming, but we have also grown and developed. It may not seem that way. The crying and fuming are more obvious.

You may have learned how to manage your finances or how to communicate more effectively. You may have been given new opportunities or developed new friendships. You've certainly developed a new level of braveness, perseverance, and determination.

God wants to gather all these skills, opportunities, and friendships and use them for our future. We don't have to leave this run-in with pornography emptyhanded. When God brought the Israelites out of slavery in Egypt, they didn't leave without something.

> "And I will make the Egyptians favorably disposed toward this people, so that when you leave you will not go empty-handed. Every woman is to ask her neighbor and any woman living in her house for articles of silver and gold and for clothing, which you will put on your sons and daughters. And so you will plunder the Egyptians."
> *Exodus 3:21-22*

The Israelites left Egypt with clothes, gold, silver, and even dough for bread. They had a forty-year camping trip ahead of them, and God was doing their packing. You and I may not have acquired silver or gold, but we have gained some treasures.

Right now, it doesn't seem like you've gained treasures. You're just trying to make it through today. And, if you're honest, it seems like the end. This could be an end. Not the end of your marriage but an end to pornography in your marriage. The end of hiding, dismissing, tolerating, and pretending. This very well could be an end. But an end is also a beginning.

I imagine the disciples thought Jesus's death was the end. Let's face it, death is pretty final when you're human. Jesus's death was an end, but it wasn't the end. His death was a beginning. The beginning of a new story for mankind. The beginning of recovering what was lost in Genesis 3.

This season, these heartaches, they're not the end for us. They're only a chapter. A bad one, mind you. But just because you and I are living in a bad chapter doesn't mean our story will have a bad ending. It might be a different ending than we thought, but it doesn't mean it's bad.

When you turn the page on this chapter, you can emerge from your forty moment, the moment life kicked our keister, equipped for the next chapter. That's what Jesus did. He spent forty days and nights fasting in the wilderness where He was tempted by Satan. He emerged victoriously. Of course, He is God. He walked out of the wilderness straight into ministry. His forty moment launched Him into ministry. The same can be true for you.

I don't mean ministry working at a church or in Africa or some far off place. I mean gathering all those treasures and ministering to people in your life. The girl in the next cubicle, the woman across the street, or your child's teacher. It could be as simple as having lunch with someone who's hurting, helping a friend work on her budget, or walking alongside another gal who is a few steps behind you.

Whatever ministry God calls you to, it starts with one thing, the same thing that started our journey together—a step. Just as you stepped onto the bridge to face the issue of pornography in your relationship, it will be one step that moves you toward ministry. But before we can step into ministry, we have to step back into life.

When my life went south, I stepped away from leading Bible study. Not because I had done anything wrong, but because I needed the mental energy and space to deal with life.

Time passed. Tears lessened. Healing happened. There eventually came a time when I was losing more than I was gaining by not leading. I needed to step back in.

If you're like me, you're waiting for life to be normal again. But what if this is your new normal? I'm not suggesting you settle for less than God's best. Don't! But sometimes life changes. Change can be hard to accept. The time eventually comes when you must accept our new normal for what it is, our new normal. Life may look different. You may look different. Different isn't bad. It's just different.

Let's embrace different and allow God to do the divine. He can make a way when there is nothing. He can create doors that never existed. He can change hearts, circumstances, and bank accounts. He is not limited by our imagination, our location, or our prayers.

We can take this space in time and allow God to do things we only dreamed of. I've always wanted to write a book. I never seriously considered putting pen to paper until pornography wrecked my marriage. If I had not gone on such a hard journey, had such an encounter with God, I may have never had the courage to write a book.

What is it for you? Dream big. What can God do with you, your story, your pain? Maybe a business is birthed, a song is written, or you finally finish your degree. God has great things He wants to do with your life. Yes, the very life you are living right now. The life that is broken, hurting, and spinning out of control. The life that seems like a lost cause some days. The life you see when you look in the mirror every morning. Yes! That life.

Let's put one foot in front of the other and step back in. We don't have to do the things we've always done. This crisis may have shown you that singing in the choir, being the room mom, gardening, or running isn't for you anymore. We're free to try new things. This crisis and these tears may have renewed your passion for creating recipes, knitting, or couponing.

Whatever step you take, God has a good future for you. You can't get there unless you keep moving forward. Not all days will be winners, but eventually the good days will outweigh the bad days and your new normal will be your regular normal.

In the meantime, we don't have to have it all figured out. Let's just do the next thing. Nothing has to be permanent. Just progress.

It takes guts to do what you've done and to keep doing what you're doing. Going to counseling, parenting your kids, being intentional. When you stepped on the bridge a few chapters ago, you never dreamed you'd be here. As you step off this bridge and into the next chapter, I hope you'll take time to glance over your shoulder and marvel at the courageous steps you've taken. Every call to courage took intention and work. You did it. You've had the guts to make choices that others may not.

Let me be the first to tell you, "Good job!"

> It's okay to be afraid, as long as your courage outweighs your fear.
>
> — ALLY LEEDS, *A NANNY FOR CHRISTMAS* MOVIE

A CALL TO COURAGE

After a time of healing and refreshment, identify specific areas where you can reengage. There is no hurry or time frame. Don't feel obligated to do the things you did before. Use some of your newly gained treasures and step back in, one baby step at a time. Start leading a Bible study again, take on a social commitment, take cupcakes to school.

ACKNOWLEDGMENTS

Back in the heyday of brick-and-mortar stores, I used to peruse bookstores marveling at all the well-constructed books. I wondered how authors put together cohesive books that challenged the mind and tugged on heart strings of readers. How did they pull that off? The answer is simple: They didn't do it alone.

That is the case with the book you hold in your hand. I didn't do it alone.

I have a sticky note on my computer that says, "My confidence lies in your faithfulness, not in my ability." That is the truest part of this book. Without the Lord, the words on these pages would still be a jumbled mess in my head. Apart from His Spirit, there is no power in well-constructed sentences or finely chosen verbs. To Him, thank you for entrusting me with this message. I didn't love living it or even writing it sometimes, but I do love sharing how You met me in the middle of it. Thank You for the opportunity to be Your voice to hurting women.

My life is better because my children challenge me to be a better mom, person, and cook. To Bennett and Grace, thank you for cheering me along in this process. Thank you for allowing me to share our story. I hope you're as proud of me as I am of you.

To my family, thank you for loving me through the mess and supporting me as I crafted this message. Holidays are the most fun days of the year because of you.

To Jenn, Kristina, Stephanie, Rosann, Megan, Rene', Michelle, Amber, Katie, Sarah, Mitzi, Tara, Brittany, Shelly, Jessica, Joy, Larry, Wendy, Deni, Alycia, and the whole First Impressions team at church. Thank you for believing in me and this book, for your keen editing eye, and for your friendship. Without your encouragement and prodding, I would still be staring at an empty screen and wallowing in a lack of confidence. Thank you for pushing me to do big things.

ABOUT THE AUTHOR

Jody Allen is a reluctant risktaker. She likes to play it safe, but several years ago she took the biggest risk of her life. After finding pornography on her home computer, she said no more. That decision led her on a path of great sorrow and, surprisingly, great joy. A path chock-full of unknowns, divorce, healing, and more risks than an introvert wants to take.

Taking a job at her church in Gastonia, North Carolina, as the Director of Women's Ministry was one of those risks. Before jumping into church ministry, Jody spent ten years as a stay-at-home mom shuffling around kids, cleaning, and searching for ways to avoid cooking.

She is a graduate of the University of North Carolina at Greensboro where she received a hard-earned and mostly deserved B.A. in Sociology.

Jody enjoys board games, deep conversations, Sunday afternoon naps, and a giant scoop of peanut butter with dark chocolate on top. Young adult twins and a dopey black lab fill her little corner of the world in North Carolina.

Invite Jody to speak at your next women's event. Your audience will be encouraged and inspired in their walk with Christ. For more information or to connect with Jody, visit **jodyallenwrites.com.**

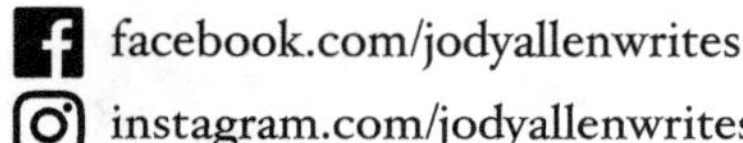

www.ingramcontent.com/pod-product-compliance
Lightning Source LLC
Chambersburg PA
CBHW061801120626
46550CB00005B/2079

* 9 7 9 8 9 9 2 0 4 6 6 0 1 *